THE GULF
WAR

Daily Express

Designed by
Start Studio
Picture research by
Sue Cranmer
**Profiles and research
by:** David Grayston
Edited by: Sylvia Barnes
and Steve Wyatt
Typeset by Diagraphic
'Typesetters Ltd London
Reproduction by
Lithospeed Ltd London
**Printed in Great
Britain** by Grosvenor
Press (Portsmouth) Ltd

CONTENTS

THE GULF WAR

'My Arab brothers, we call you to a Holy War. Do not hesitate. Stand up against the outrage of foreign troops in our lands and you will find victory. All believers in Allah, wherever you are, this is your day to rise up.'

— *Saddam Hussein* —

OIL... AND A MAN WITH A VISION OF DESTINY

The name of Saddam Hussein and the nature of his regime first came to widespread notice in Britain during Iraq's bloody eight-year war against Iran which ended on August 20, 1988. But he became a household name after the arrest and execution of Observer journalist Farzad Bazoft in March 1990.

Bazoft had been invited to Iraq as a guest of the Government, but he fatally chose to investigate reports that 700 had died in an explosion at a secret experimental missile plant in Al Iskanderia, 20 miles south of Baghdad.

Bazoft, an exiled Iranian and opponent of the Ayatollahs, was picked up by Iraq's Mukhabarat secret police as he tried to fly out of the country. Following a televised confession he was hanged as an Israeli spy in spite of mercy pleas from many World leaders.

After the widespread outrage over Bazoft's death things calmed down. Whatever they said at the time, most Western governments went back to business as usual with Iraq. But the calm was illusory, for Saddam was laying the groundwork for his invasion of Kuwait.

With hindsight, his actions were dictated by a remorseless logic. Saddam saw himself as a man of destiny, born to lead the Arabs. It was this that had led him into the disastrous invasion of non-Arab Iran. If he had won he would have dominated the region and been able to dictate the price of oil.

The brutal war decimated the economies of both countries. If he was to achieve his aim he would have to find another way that would enable him first to rebuild Iraq's treasury through higher oil prices and then to dominate the Gulf. Saddam began to lean on the other members of OPEC, demanding a reduction on oil production until the price had risen to $25 a barrel from the then level of $17. OPEC would only agree to a rise to $21, nowhere near enough to enable Saddam to rebuild an economy nobody else wanted to invest in.

So on July 17, 1990, Saddam began rattling the sabre at his tiny neighbour Kuwait. The excuse was a long-running dispute over the ownership of the Rumaila oilfield on the border between the two countries.

The Iraqi President accused Kuwait's ruling family of conspiring to bring down the price of OPEC oil by exceeding production quotas, stealing Iraqi oil from the shared Rumaila field and other border violations. He stepped up his war of words by demanding all of the Rumaila field, border changes, compensation of $2.4 billion for "stolen" oil and a write-off of the $12 billion that Kuwait had lent to Iraq during the Gulf war.

Saddam backed these demands by moving 30,000 of his crack troops and 200 tanks to the border.

The Arab states made desperate diplomatic attempts to stop an invasion, with Egyptian president Hosni Mubarak and King Hussein of Jordan to the fore. Less than two weeks before Iraqi tanks rolled down the highway to Kuwait City, Mubarak said he had a personal promise from Saddam that he would not use force. His fury at the lie partially explains Egypt's subsequent hawkish stance against Iraq.

On July 25, Kuwait's Crown Prince Sheikh Sa'ad al-Sabah offered talks to Saddam. Those talks were held in the Saudi port of Jedda. They broke down on July 31. Iraq invaded on August 2 and the tragic story that followed was to touch the hearts and minds of millions across the globe.

CHAPTER 1

THE GULF WAR

AT 2AM on August 2, 1990, the still of the desert was broken by a roar. Dust swirled in the darkness as 350 Iraqi tanks lumbered from their holes in the sand and headed for the Al-Abdaly border checkpoint and the road to Kuwait City, doorway to the dunes that held a rich prize...100 billion barrels of oil.

Saddam Hussein had finally drawn the sabre he had been rattling over 17 days of relentless military, moral and megaphone diplomacy. He was invading his tiny neighbour.

It was no contest. Kuwait City, a 90-mile square toytown of air-conditioned hotels, marble banks and ostentatious public buildings, had 20,000 defenders under arms. Saddam had a million troops equipped with 5,500 battle tanks more than Britain and France put together 450 artillery pieces and multiple rocket launchers, 510 combat aircraft and 160 helicopter gunships.

The spearhead of this mammoth military machine came down the 50-mile, six-lane highway to the heart of Kuwait City, dropping off troops on the way to seal intersections. A nightmare that the West, moderate Arab states and Israel had feared was coming true. Saddam, the Sunni Moslem who claimed descent from Nebuchadnezzar, the ancient king of Mesopotamia who destroyed Jerusalem and enslaved the Jews, was launched upon his dream to rule the Middle East and become a 20th Century Caliph of Baghdad.

The first men to realise that this was really war were the lorry drivers dragged from their trucks at gunpoint and taken prisoner 10 miles short of the border on the Iraqi side. They stood frightened and bewildered on the roadside, watching the tanks thunder by.

Saddam had chosen his elite Republican Guard to lead the assault on the desert emirate.

'Any power, big or small that intervenes will have its arm cut off!'

Baghdad Radio

They had borne the brunt of the bloody war against Iran and were still totally loyal to him.

At the Al-Abdaly checkpoint, an undistinguished clump of low concrete buildings, customs and immigration officials dozed or played cards. One stepped out into the darkness, sure he had heard the rumbling of heavy machinery. Mortars exploded around him. Dozens of tanks crashed through the flimsy red and white wooden barrier.

He and his frightened colleagues had time to make one telephone call to Kuwait City before troops burst through the door and sprayed the room with machine gun fire.

All along the 200-mile border there were similar scenes as the tanks crashed into Kuwait. Ahead of them squads of Saddam's special forces were airlifted into the capital aboard helicopter gunships, securing road junctions and other key positions.

The Kuwaiti troops were outnumbered 50 to 1. What few tanks they had were strung out around the grounds of the ornate Dasman Palace, home of the Emir of Kuwait, 62-year old Sheikh Jabar al-Ahmed al-Sabah. His family, one of the richest in the world, had ruled the state for 200 years.

The Emir's Royal Guard was preparing a brave last stand at the palace overlooking the waters of the Gulf. It was to be the scene of the fiercest fighting in the three-hour blitzkrieg invasion.

Within 30 minutes of the attack Kuwait Radio interrupted music programmes with a frantic statement from the Ministry of Defence. "We did not expect Iraq to do this!" shouted the announcer, his voice breaking with emotion. "We implore them to stop such an irresponsible action and reserve the right to use all legitimate means to repel them. We shall die but Kuwait will live. We will make the aggressors taste the chalice of death!"

His words, moving but futile, were answered by a brief moment of Kuwaiti glory. At Mutla, 25 miles north of the capital, one of its fighter jets shot down an Iraqi helicopter. The jet wheeled in the night sky as it bore down on another gunship, but was chased away by artillery fire from the ground.

By 3.30am the Iraqi tanks were on the outskirts of the capital. Kuwait Radio stayed on the air, playing martial music and pleading with its citizens to fight on the streets. It begged forlornly for its Arab "brothers" in the Gulf to ride to the rescue.

As the blood-red sun lifted above the horizon, a wave of Iraqi Migs flew over the city, pounding the palace grounds with rocket fire. Saddam's tanks and stormtroopers moved in, inflicting more than 200 casualties among the Emir's loyal guard. Among the many dead was his 45-year-old younger half-brother, Sheikh Fahad, fatally wounded on the steps of the palace. The Emir fled by helicopter to Saudi Arabia.

Behind him tanks surrounded the British and American embassies. An Iraqi jet squadron headed for the airport to the west of Kuwait City. The sonic booms as they crashed through the sound barrier spread panic. Black smoke billowed from fuel dumps and shattered buildings. Even as the Emir and his immediate family were making their escape Iraqi troops were bearing down on the state Central Bank. One brave clerk frantically worked fax and telephone lines, transferring billions of pounds in assets out of the country. Two guards died as the soldiers burst into the building. The clerk managed to escape.

The day dawned on a terrifying scene. The Iraqis were in control of key military installations, public buildings and the disputed Rumaila oilfields on the northern border. Thousands of Kuwaitis and expatriate Britons, Americans, Germans and Russians were trying to flee to Saudi Arabia but tanks and troops had encircled the capital and sealed off the roads. They found themselves prisoners in their own homes.

A recorded message at the British Embassy told them: "Stock up with food and stay indoors." Envoys ordered Britons to "keep their heads down and stay out of trouble". With a curfew announced and communication links virtually severed, they could do nothing else.

The Iraqi troops, many of them simple village Arabs who had long resented their sophisticated neighbours' conspicuous wealth, took their revenge. They shot out the plate glass windows of expensive stores along Fahd Salem Street and helped themselves to souvenirs. Iraqi generals rode around in impounded Rolls-Royces. Stories of rape spread through the capital.

The Kuwaiti royal family managed to make television appeals from Saudi Arabia. A picture of the Prime Minister appeared briefly on Kuwaiti television screens. "We shall clean treachery from our land," he vowed.

Baghdad Radio gave its version of events. Kuwait's younger generation, fed up with royal rulers bleeding their country dry, had seized control in a brilliant coup and asked Saddam for help, it said. The Iraqi leader had set up the "Free Provisional Kuwait Government".

KUWAIT: A GLITTERING JEWEL THAT ROSE FROM THE SAN

'This is the blackest day in the history of the Arabs.'

Cairo's Al-Ahram newspaper

In their first broadcast the "Free Provisional Kuwait Government" dissolved Kuwait's National Assembly, shut ports and airports and announced an indefinite curfew. They claimed they had sacked the Emir and his followers for being "traitors and agents of Zionist and foreign powers".

As dusk fell on August 2 pockets of Kuwaiti troops were refusing to surrender. They sniped at Iraqi units and sporadic gunfire could be heard throughout the city. Outside the Dasman Palace half a dozen Iraqi armoured personnel carriers were burning. The Iraqis admitted that 85 of their troops had been wounded, though eyewitnesses reported bodies left on the streets untended for hours. Kuwaiti officials said up to 200 of their men had been killed.

Saddam, the peasant boy who picked up his first gun at 10 and killed his first man at 19, threatened to turn Kuwait into a graveyard if anyone tried to stop his takeover. Whatever happened now, the 53-year-old ruler of Iraq had already marched into history.

otlines were buzzing. The Iraqis were perfectly capable of crashing through to take Saudi Arabia and the fat, defenceless Gulf states. Sheikhdoms from Bahrain to Oman trembled.

Kuwait had ceased to exist except as a money pump and a 200-mile coastline to enhance the already formidable power of Saddam's almost landlocked domain. Kuwait's oil reserves were the third largest in the non-Communist world.

In New York diplomats scoured the city rounding up ambassadors for an emergency meeting of the UN Security Council. The invasion presented them with an immense challenge. Saddam had flouted the UN Charter in pushing his troops across an internationally-agreed border and in removing the Emir by force. Already, behind the scenes, Britain and America were pushing for sanctions.

Mrs Thatcher and President Bush held a quick council of war in Aspen, Colorado. They called on their allies to make Iraq an international outcast and stop its oil. US Secretary of State James Baker flew straight to Moscow to discuss the crisis. The Kremlin banned arms deliveries to Iraq. Kuwait's UN ambassador called for military intervention from the West. Britain's Foreign Secretary Douglas Hurd gave Iraq 48 hours to get out of Kuwait or face "fresh action". Even in these early hours of the crisis both Britain and America were contemplating the prospect of using military force.

As the UN Security Council unanimously condemned the attack, the Iraqi ambassador announced: "We hope this will last just a matter of days, or weeks at the most." Few believed him.

Saddam's armoured brigades stood at the doors of Saudi Arabia. Spanning a forbidding 830,000 square miles of barren terrain, an area almost as big as Europe, the kingdom floated on a sea of oil the West needed to survive.

The Saudis had thought themselves immune from invasion, buying off potential aggressors with their almost limitless wealth. The country had been run as a virtual family business by the

WHERE ONCE THE ONLY ENEMY WAS A DESERT DUST STORM

Until the invasion Kuwait City was a glittering, modern metropolis rising from barren sand. Now it is wrecked.

Kuwait was named after the Arab word for fort, kut. The state is virtually flat desert, the highest point 991ft above sea level.

The country covers an area of 6,880 square miles and the average temperature is 91F, although it can rise to 126F. Rainfall is negligible, ranging from 1 to 7 inches a year.

The soil, if that is the word, is not suitable for farming. Fierce dust storms can rage for days. Less than nine per cent of the land is arable and most vegetation is scrubland.

The main sources of water for the 1.7 million people of Kuwait are five desalination plants which produce 215 million gallons of fresh water a day from the sea.

Most of the population 99 per cent live in towns and cities on the country's coastal strip. They speak Arabic and are overwhelmingly Moslem, with 78 per cent from the orthodox Sunni sect and 14 per cent of the more radical Shias.

Until the invasion native Kuwaiti Arabs numbered less than half the country's population. There were five main layers in the social structure of the country ranging from the ruling family down through the old-established merchant families Bedouins who had forsaken their nomadic lives in favour of life in the city naturalised Arabs from other countries, white expatriates and an underclass of Third World menials. Less than 25 per cent of the workforce were natives, and most of those worked for the government.

Kuwait has huge oil reserves the third largest in the non-Communist world and these served to give Kuwaitis one of the highest standards of living in the world.

Oil was the only industry of any significance. Kuwait produced 91 million tonnes in 1989 compared to 138 million tonnes for vastly bigger Iraq over the same period.

Kuwait was also a very valuable trading partner for Britain. In 1989 we imported goods, including oil, worth £150 million from Kuwait whilst our exports to them were worth £228 million.

Until Saddam's troops stormed across the border Kuwait was a constitutional monarchy ruled by the al-Sabah family, whose dynasty was established in 1756. In 1914 Britain recognised Kuwait as an independent country under British protection, but it was not until 1961 that the emirate achieved full independence. After the August 2 invasion Saddam declared it the 19th province of Iraq and named it after himself.

King Fahd of Saudi Arabia. Now he had to defend his own borders

prolific al-Sauds, who had seized control from among the ruins of the Ottoman Empire. They operated a closed Moslem state, turning their backs on the fluctuating fortunes of the rest of the region. But while they fenced themselves in, they could not fence the real world out.

The Saudis, under King Fahd, had more money than Iraq. But like Kuwait they had a pathetically inadequate army – an expensively-equipped force of 66,000 Palestinian and Pakistani exiles, who had made the country their home.

Fahd had long been aware of the threat from his neighbour. He had only bankrolled the Iraqi leader's war with Iran because he feared Teheran's mullahs more. Fahd was now too old and infirm with a heart condition to try to play the Saviour of the Arab world himself. It looked as though he would have to settle for defending his own kingdom's borders. The telephone lines were burning between Riyadh, the Foreign Office and the Pentagon.

Turkey too was in the front line, vulnerable because of the Iraqi oil pipeline which passed through the country to the coast carrying a million tons of Iraqi oil every week. Istanbul would provoke its powerful neighbour if it joined a world economic protest by it closing down.

And then there was Israel, the nuclear-armed wild card in the Middle East pack. How would the Israelis react?

They were no friends of Saddam Hussein, to be sure. In June 1981 they had bombed an Iraqi nuclear reactor outside Baghdad, fearing that its real purpose was to produce the plutonium for nuclear weapons. Since then Saddam had threatened to reduce Israel to a chemical wasteland. It was feared in Whitehall that Iraq was still trying to achieve a nuclear capability in co-operation with Libya. Hours after the invasion of Kuwait Israeli President Yitzhak Shamir reminded the West and even his Arab foes that they should take such possibilities seriously.

But there was also the Palestinian issue, the running sore of the region. Saddam's supporters, with some justification, asked how the West could condemn Iraq's occupation of Kuwait while seemingly condoning Israel's continued occupation of the West Bank and Gaza and the Israelis' treatment of the Arabs therein. They saw the outcry as yet another example of the ever-imperialist West's hypocrisy.

The scenario was a diplomatic nightmare. But President Bush took a deep breath and warned that any further aggression by Saddam could trigger outright war.

On the steps of his home in the Colorado sunshine, with Mrs Thatcher by his side, he condemned the invasion and called for the immediate withdrawal of Iraqi forces.

"We are committed to taking whatever steps are necessary to safeguard our long-standing interests in the Gulf and protecting American citizens if they are put in harm's way," he said. "Mrs Thatcher and I are concerned about naked aggression."

His pledge to protect American citizens was no mere rhetoric. Thousands of American and British, and other citizens were at risk, caught in the invasion and wondering what their fate would be. Saddam had hostages.

Among them were 367 British Airways passengers, 11 of them children, stranded at Kuwait airport on board the Boeing 747 Coniston Water. The jumbo had been delayed leaving Heathrow. By 3am on the morning of August 2 it should have been safely refuelled and long gone from Kuwait but Iraqi fighters screamed in to strafe the runway as the flight engineer was running through his departure checks. With 200 tonnes of fuel aboard the pilot had no choice but to abandon take-off. His passengers fled in their in-flight slippers.

Further tension arose after reports of American workers being rounded up in the Kuwaiti oilfields and taken away "for their own safety". They had not been seen since.

There were fears too for the safety of 35 British servicemen seized in their homes by Iraqi troops in Kuwait and taken to Baghdad. The servicemen were members of an RAF technical liaison team providing back-up for equipment supplied to Kuwait's defence force.

The hostage situation was beginning to loom large in everyone's mind, but many experts were convinced that Britons and Americans would not be harmed by Iraqi troops. One diplomat said: "There is a strong anti-British, anti-American movement in Iraq but it would serve them no purpose to harm foreigners."

Pentagon officials, trying to calm war fears, said US Marines would only go in if the 4,000 Americans in the invasion zone were in danger.

Militarily the few American and British forces in the Gulf at the time could do little but offer a presence. So began the diplomatic arm-twisting for a trade ban. In theory Iraq, even with Kuwait added, was not the most difficult of countries to isolate. Its own meagre port facilities were all at the upper end of the narrow Shatt al-Arab waterway and the Gulf itself was an easily-blockaded cul de sac.

The bulk of the oil which constituted Iraq's only real source of wealth could only be exported in any quantity through two pipelines, the one crossing Turkey and another through Saudi Arabia. Removing even the combined Kuwaiti-

Iraqi oil contribution from the international market would not, for the moment, create an embarrassing shortage. Even water, on which a near-desert economy like Iraq was heavily dependent, could offer leverage.

But there was a difference between listing such options and turning them into effective means of persuasion. So much was apparent only hours after the invasion.

n the day of the invasion hundreds of Kuwaitis gathered outside their embassy in Queen's Gate in a sweltering 90F heatwave, carrying pictures of the deposed Emir and chanting: "Our blood is heating to die for our Motherland!"

World oil prices leapt and more than £6 billion was wiped off share values, with the FT Index tumbling 34.5 points. There were more falls on the Tokyo and New York exchanges. Only gold prospered, as always in times of troubles, the bullion price jumping $7.45 to $380.70 an ounce.

Following America's lead the Treasury and the Bank of England froze £15 billion of Kuwaiti assets in the UK to prevent Saddam taking a stake in some of Britain's biggest companies. It was seen as the strongest commercial weapon the Government could wield against the Iraqis, who had no British assets of their own due to rock-bottom diplomatic relations over recent years. The Treasury move was made after requests from the Kuwaiti ambassador in London. Britain had not frozen the assets of a country since Argentina invaded the Falklands in 1982. The Stock Exchange, also froze all share transactions involving the Kuwaiti government and its citizens.

The clampdown threw the spotlight on the little-known but extremely powerful Kuwaiti Investment Office in London. It had £15 billion invested in UK shares and property, including a stake in BP worth £1.7 billion, as well as 10.5 per cent of the Midland Bank. The Kuwaitis, with an estimated £50 billion invested worldwide, had been operating the KIO for nearly 30 years, building up investments to provide long-term wealth for the Gulf state. In Britain they owned over 11 per cent of travel agency Hogg Robinson, 10 per cent of hotel group Mount Charlotte and big stakes in three large Lloyds insurance brokers.

The Kuwaitis were good for business in other areas. They spent tens of millions a year in British stores and on luxury homes in London. The value of their flats and houses in the capital was put at £500 million. Many were within shopping distance of Harrods.

Even whinnies of alarm were being raised among the racing fraternity in Newmarket, a town reliant on Arab patronage. The Arabs had almost total control over the best horses, trainers and breeding stock. There the Sport of Kings had been renamed the Sport of Sheikhs. The Kuwaiti Emir's brother, Sheikh Fahad, who had died in the fighting around Dasman Palace, owned the 1982 Royal Ascot winner, Mubarak of Kuwait.

Dubai's ruling family, the Maktoums, had poured £2 billion into British racing. About a third of their 1,000 horses were trained in Newmarket, where they owned five studs

IRAQ: A MAGNET FOR CONQUERORS FROM THE BEGINNING OF TIME

The fabled Silk Road to China ran through Baghdad. When Marco Polo took the Golden Path to Samarkand, this was the way he came.

Trade and the fertility of its fields made Iraq, then called Mesopotamia, a magnet for conquerors from the earliest times.

Whenever war overtook the world Mesopotamia became a battleground for the major powers. The fates of Britain and Iraq have been linked since 1914 when troops from Britain's Indian Army landed in the Gulf.

Peace came in November 1918. Britain occupied the country, with a mandate to rule under the treaty which ended the Great War.

In November 1930 Britain granted independence to Iraq, supporting her country's admission to the League of Nations in 1932.

But only after almost 40 years of chronic instability, with governments and revolutions following in bewildering succession, did peace finally come to Iraq.

On July 17, 1968, a group of Right-wing officers from the Arab Socialist Renaissance Party, Ba'ath, took over led by General al Bakr.

Saddam Hussein soon emerged as the strongman behind the scenes. He seized power in July 1979 and his reign began with the executions of more than 500 Ba'ath party members in two weeks.

Iraq had finally found the leader who could give her stability and expansion. The price was a police state.

One policy common to all Iraqi regimes was hatred of Israel, and the Iraqis joined with the other Arab states in the unsuccessful wars of 1965 and 1973.

The Israelis in turn recognised Iraq as an implacable enemy and in 1981 they destroyed what was claimed to be an almost-completed nuclear reactor which the French were helping to build at Dimona.

In an historic miscalculation Saddam invaded Iran and by the time both sides accepted a UN ceasefire in 1988 millions had died, including more than 500,000 Iraqis, and the economies of both countries had been smashed.

Iraq's desperate need to quell dissent and rebuild itself led to the use of chemical weapons on Kurdish civilians and to Saddam's attempt to bounce OPEC into raising oil prices to $25 a barrel. Their refusal made the invasion of Kuwait inevitable.

The Emir of Kuwait. He fled to the safety of Saudi Arabia

including the giant Dalham Hall complex, home to several of Europe's most valuable stallions. Leading owner Sheikh Mohammed al-Maktoum had returned to the Gulf to fulfil his duties as Defence Minister of the United Arab Emirates. His three brothers Maktoum, Hamdan and Ahmed had joined him in Dubai, 400 miles down the Gulf from Kuwait. Everyone was worried that the crisis would escalate into full-blown war.

The immediate concern for the West was undoubtedly economic. Saddam wanted OPEC to resume the militancy of the early 1970s when, with their hand on the tap, the producers had the industrial world over an oil barrel. If oil prices spiralled again inflationary pressures could tip the world towards recession. Petrol prices were soaring and Britain's inflation rate was threatening to top 10 per cent. North Sea oil exceeded $30 a barrel.

But there were other voices trying to allay the panic. Britain could take heart, they said, that dearer oil would encourage the West to use it more sparingly to the benefit of the environment. North Sea production, already almost a third more than Kuwait's at some two million barrels a day, would be boosted. And Britain was a world leader in oil exploration technology. Dearer oil would trigger an upturn in the global hunt for new sources, lifting a major sector of the English and Scottish economies.

The West was suddenly patting itself on the back that it had a near-record 99 days of oil stocks and plentiful output. The £ managed to keep its nerve as money flooded into the dollar, the traditional haven in times of crisis.

There was another considerable source of comfort. The Cold War was over. There seemed little prospect of a Middle East war flaring into a superpower conflict, as would have been almost inevitable a decade earlier. The nuclear missiles slept in their silos.

he inquest began. In Washington, a secret war was raging. The CIA was busy defending itself in the wake of the disastrous events. It claimed that Western officials had been adequately informed of Saddam's military build-up and of the threat of war. It took the unusual step of issuing a public statement, denying that its reports on the Iraqi military were inadequate or ambiguous.

"We provided policy makers with very useful and timely information on these events. There were no surprises," said spokesman Mark Mansfield.

The implication was that the CIA had done its job and the politicians had failed to act on information given. It appeared true that American satellite photographs of Iraqi troop dispositions over the days preceding the invasion were so precise that CIA director William Webster was able to tell Brent Scowcroft, the White House national security adviser, precisely how many Iraqi soldiers were gathered on the Kuwait border, how many tanks they had and where they were located.

Webster, it was claimed, even warned Scowcroft that the Iraqi forces were capable of swiftly taking over Kuwait and driving straight

THE BEDOUIN WHO EARNED A MILLION POUNDS A MINUTE

Every minute he earned a tax-free million pounds. He was forty times richer than the Queen, herself the World's richest woman. He gave Princess Diana a diamond necklace worth a million pounds as a small token of his esteem.

He was Sheikh Jabar Ahmed al-Sabah, Emir of Kuwait since 1977; one of the richest men ever to have lived, but a Bedouin who set little store by possessions.

His family ruled Kuwait from 1756, but until an assassination bid in 1989 the 63-year-old Emir visited the Kuwait bazaar on foot for his shopping. He had a score of palaces, but worried more about the welfare of his subjects than spending his incalculable wealth.

He could have spent his time anywhere, but preferred his small desert kingdom. The Emir's favourite holiday was not Monaco or Davos, but sailing or fishing on Failaka Island off Kuwait's coast.

He had done everything to bring Western benefits to his subjects, from a welfare state to a modern transport system, and glitzy hotels, but he, like them, was at heart an Arab who loved the desert wilderness.

The Emirs of Kuwait were never absolute rulers, preferring to share power with the merchant classes. But they were careful to retain the string of power in their hands.

Since the country became independent in 1914, the throne was shared by the families of the two sons of modern Kuwait's founder Mubarak the Great – Jabar and Salem.

Whenever an Emir died his successor was elected by an assembly of the country's nobles and ruling classes. But the Royal Family always retained control of the country's key posts – Defence, Home Affairs and Foreign affairs – and family members always made up at least a quarter of the Cabinet.

The West has often seen Arab princes as playboys who were happy to waste huge amounts of money in Europe's fleshpots but who ruled with a rod of iron at home.

Sheikh Jabar was neither. When his distant relatives on the fringes of the extended Kuwaiti royal family flaunted their wealth in London's West End he was embarrassed.

To a constitutional monarch who believed neither in corporal nor capital punishment, Saddam Hussein's rape of Kuwait came as a profound shock. Some have suggested that his ancestors, who shared no such scruples, would have been better prepared.

on to Saudi Arabia. The American intelligence failure was, it seemed, one of interpretation, not information.

According to The Independent newspaper in Britain the US administration had trusted assurances Saddam gave to both American officials and Arab leaders such as Egyptian president Hosni Mubarak.

One of the more embarrassing errors was made by April Glaspie, the US ambassador to Baghdad. Saddam had called her a few days before the invasion and assured her that his differences with Kuwait, were purely an Arab "family row". She felt sufficiently confident to leave Baghdad for a summer holiday shortly afterwards.

In London the pre-war assessment seemed to have been that Iraq was engaged in warmongering diplomacy designed to squeeze more cash out of its rich Kuwaiti neighbour and that an invasion was a non-starter. The assessment was apparently reached on the basis of the same US technical intelligence.

How wrong it was.

On August 4, two days after the invasion, the remnants of Kuwait's pocket army were fighting a valiant last stand against Saddam's stormtroopers. Kuwaiti diplomats reported that more than 1,000 of their troops and civilians had been killed.

Battles were raging in Kuwait City and in the vast oilfields running to the Saudi border as Saddam's mopping-up continued. Thousands of Britons were still trapped inside their homes and hotel basements, cowering under relentless shellfire. Iraqi gunboats and artillery units were bombarding the capital's diplomatic enclave, trying to crush the last resistance.

Kuwaiti troops were holed up inside an army barracks at Shuwaikh, north of the capital near the royal palace. The British embassy was caught in the crossfire though none of the 22 staff were hurt. Embassy official David McDonough, in a telephone call to London, said: "Burning tanks are littering the streets. There are two either side of our building."

Passengers from the British Airways jet Coniston Water were spending a second night in hotel basements as mortar fire crashed around them.

Iraqi gunboats were concentrating on seizing ports along the Kuwaiti coast and helicopter-borne troops overran oilfields south of Kuwait City. They dug in half a mile from the Saudi border.

In the days that followed the trickle of reports from Kuwait turned into a flood. Iraqi officers had taken over the Sheraton Hotel for their

KUWO1:KUWAIT,KUWAIT, 2AUG90 - Iraqi tanks line up along the coastline August 2, facing the sea near the Salmya district of Kuwait where they fired at Kuwaiti naval vessels offshore. Iraqi forces invaded Kuwait early Aug 2 sending Sheikh Al-Sabah into exile in neighbouring Saudi Arabia.Editors note: Photo made from photographer croached behind balcony (foreground).
       mal/str   REUTER

Beach frontline: Iraqi tanks blast Kuwaiti gunboats from the city shore

headquarters, ignoring government buildings and choosing to direct their invasion in comfort.

Most of the city's residents were sitting tight at home. There was some panic-buying in supermarkets. In one area of the city Kuwaitis queued for videos to help see them through the siege. Iraqi troops drove around the capital in confiscated police cars. Already Britons were going into hiding in attics, cupboards, empty water tanks and behind false walls.

One of the most graphic accounts of the invasion of Kuwait City came from British merchant banker Kevin Hayden, one of a brave band of 30 Britons who defied Iraqi tanks and guns to make a dash for freedom dash across the desert.

Kevin, 31, his Singaporean wife Sulianah and their friend Bob Grimstead were woken by gunfire on the day of the invasion. Their flat was opposite the Emir's palace.

"It was horrific," said Kevin. "The palace and the embassies were surrounded by tanks. We did not know what the hell was going on. All along the Kuwaitis had said, 'Don't worry, everything will be all right. There won't be an invasion'.

"We poked our heads up to see out of the window. The Iraqis spotted us. They obviously thought we were snipers or look-outs so they opened fire.

"The shots smashed the picture window at the front of the apartment and two at the side. One of the bullets shattered the bathroom ceiling. It splintered and pieces of lead embedded themselves in my wife's back.

"There was glass everywhere and I was

Beach prisoners. Civilians, including Britons and Americans are held on the shoreline during the early hours of the invasion

covered in shards. It was four days before I managed to get all the pieces out. There was a lot of blood.

"From time to time Bob and I kept peering through the shattered windows to see what was happening.

"We saw three Iraqi tanks, big ones, come around the corner of the palace followed by hundreds of troops. They were firing at the grounds. The Iraqi troops dug in.

"Later four smaller Kuwaiti tanks arrived. The Iraqi troops fired at them but were mown down. There were snipers in nearby buildings and the Kuwaitis began to shoot at them. Finally the Kuwaiti tanks were blown up.

"The fighting went on for about five hours. At one time I saw Iraqi soldiers standing guard over a group of between two and three hundred civilians they had rounded up.

"They were pointing guns at them. Most of the prisoners had their hands up. The soldiers took them down to the beach, then some Kuwaiti troops appeared and began shooting at the Iraqis. The Iraqis scattered, fleeing down to the sea. They were running in every direction. The civilians managed to get away and four of them ran into the British embassy.

"Three times the Iraqis attacked the palace. They were beaten off every time. There were many dead. We met two surgeons who told us many Kuwaitis were arriving dead in hospital."

Kevin and his group of friends decided to get out. Their eight-car convoy, two pregnant women and eight children among the escapees, was guided by a Kuwaiti helper across ancient Bedouin tracks to the Saudi border. The Kuwaiti then turned back to help others.

It took 18 hours to reach the safety of Bahrain. During the desert dash they saw Iraqi tanks shelling other refugees who were making similar bids for freedom.

Londoner Adrian King, 34, said: "It was a pretty hairy adventure. But when we heard of the escalation we decided it was high time to go whatever the risk. We all got in and made off.

"God knows what route we took. We just followed our Kuwaiti saviour. He was bloody marvellous. He would not take any money. He simply showed us the way to the border then left. God bless him.

"Sometimes we took well-worn tracks and roads, sometimes we made off across the sand to get away from Iraqi patrols.

"We went as fast as we could but often we were crawling through sand nearly two feet deep. Once we stopped to go back to help another car which got stuck.

"It was a tense, frightening journey. But everyone was terribly British. No tears, no panic. We just drove like hell through the night and stayed together."

There were reports that the invading Iraqi troops had raped dozens of women.

Mrs Anne King from Worthing in Surrey said: "We had seen an Iraqi soldier walking around our block of flats. My next door neighbour was on her own with three children and this soldier had come round and knocked on her door with his gun. She just picked up the three kids, ran out the back door and came to us.

"I looked out of the window and saw the soldier walking out of the front gate. I didn't think any more about it until an hour later when my maid came in and told me an Iraqi soldier was about.

"I went into another apartment and found that my neighbour had been raped. The soldier had tied her German husband up and raped the wife, then made them sit down and have a cup of tea with him."

Another story was of Filipino women being raped at a compound for foreign domestic staff.

"The Iraqis went from door to door," said Dominador Miradora, 40, an oil refinery worker who managed to surface safely in Manila. "They locked all of us men in the toilet, then picked the women of their fancy and raped them. We heard the women screaming and weeping but what could we do? They had guns."

Another invasion eyewitness, British engineer Neil MacDonald, was woken by the sound of gunfire in the night at the small oil complex of Abuhalifa, 20 miles north of Kuwait City.

The 35-year-old former soldier ran from his apartment just in time to see Iraqi jets hit a nearby communications centre. Realising that the invasion he had feared for weeks was under way he grabbed his wife Eleanor and two-year-old son Scott and rounded up his colleagues.

With only a few possessions including Scott's teddy bear he led a 13-truck convoy across the desert to the Saudi border, two hours away, trying to dodge the Iraqi tanks and troops swarming into the country.

The convoy picked up fleeing Bedouin families along the way and suffered frightening moments having passports checked by Iraqi commanders in Jeeps.

On Monday August 6, as the UN took its historic vote in favour of mandatory economic and arms sanctions against Iraq, Neil flew into Heathrow.

"Something needed to be done when the bombs started dropping," he said. "They were very, very close. We saw the Iraqi jets screaming overhead. Then we heard the thuds and saw the damage as they hit their targets. I put together a convoy and got the hell out of there."

Eleanor, 37, added: "We just took our son and his teddy and headed for safety. We are grateful to be alive."

Another daring escape was planned not far from Saddam's Baghdad palace. Sixteen Britons in the Sheraton Hotel had just heard that the border with Jordan was open. Each chipped in £200 to hire a convoy of six taxis to take them the 600 miles across the treacherous and desolate Badimatt Ash Shum region to the frontier. It was a gamble that could cost them their lives. The desert was alive with Iraqi patrols, trigger-happy following reports that US forces were arriving in Saudi Arabia.

The fugitives, with no protection against the 120F heat, made it to the ramshackle Iraqi border post of Al Ruswayshid, its 75-foot red and white radio tower a welcoming sight.

But the Jordanian border was still 50 miles away across a lunar no-man's land of craters and rocks baked black by the sun.

Andrew Thompson, 44, from Solihull, told how the escapees faced an agonising hour's wait as their passports were taken away and checked for exit visas by armed guards.

"It was terrifying," he said. "We were stuck there without our passports and had no idea whether they would even be given back or what would happen to us.

"The guards eventually waved us through and our taxi drivers having made a handsome profit sped back to Baghdad. We were just left there in the middle of the desert with our cases.

"We still had 50 miles to go so I plucked up courage and went up to one of the Iraqi guards to explain our position. He smiled, so I gave him some dinars and to my amazement he stepped out onto the road and started to flag down some rusting Jordanian vegetable trucks.

"We just jumped on the back of them and hitched a ride to freedom. God knows what would have happened if the guard hadn't taken those dinars."

There were emotional scenes at the Jordanian border post, a former oil pumping station known as H4, as the men realised they were safe. They hugged each other in tears when they caught their first glimpse of the Union Jack Flag in a coach which had been sent to meet them.

They were greeted by Major Mike Phillips from the British Embassy. He gave them fresh fruit and mineral water, quickly gulped down by the weary travellers. More than 100 Jordanian police watched in amazement as the Britons

Pied Pier of Kuwait, Neil MacDonald and son, Scott

President Bush and Mrs Thatcher. Their military build-up was already underway

cheered and broke into Land of Hope and Glory.

Other fugitives weren't so lucky. Soon after the convoy's escape the curtain came down on Westerners fleeing through the checkpoint, even though Saddam had promised to keep the freedom corridor open for families caught up in the conflict. Hundreds of British families came tantalisingly close to freedom only to see it snatched away when Iraqis ordered them off their coaches at gunpoint and made them return.

A Filipino businessman told Daily Express reporter Paul Thompson that he saw groups of Britons forced to sit on the ground under the blazing sun waiting for transport back to Baghdad.

"There was nothing that could be done," he said. "We all felt sorry for them but no one wanted to get involved. They were grouped together and forced to sit on the floor. If they moved they would be shot by armed guards around them."

A tearful Lebanese family, the Hassans, were fleeing for of all places Beirut. Jamil Hassan, 34, said: "We are returning to Beirut because it is our home. We will be safe there."

In Whitehall the Foreign Office exposed Saddam's "freedom corridor" as a sham. Only Westerners with valid exit visas were being allowed to travel. The Britons bussed from Kuwait to Baghdad after the invasion did not have the entry visas necessary to get exit visas. It was a bureaucratic Catch 22.

Western diplomats were sceptical that Saddam would throw away his greatest trump card in the Middle East war of nerves his hostages. A British embassy official in the Gulf said: "Although Saddam might well be ready to release some foreigners it would be foolish to think he will let everyone go. The hostages in Baghdad are his best insurance policy against a counter-attack."

He was right. Saddam's puppet regime in Kuwait said it would retaliate against trapped foreigners if the West imposed sanctions. The nine-man military junta, headed by Saddam's son-in-law Colonel Ali, blatantly threatened the safety of the British and American communities.

"These countries should not expect us to behave honourably at a time when they are conspiring against us and our brothers in Iraq in an aggressive way," said the regime's mouthpiece, the Voice of the Masses Radio.

The threat was driven home by the desert murder of Briton Douglas Croskery. The 49-year-old print company manager was gunned down two miles from the Saudi border as he tried to help a convoy of families escape the war zone. Troops dragged him from his car, shot him with a Kalashnikov rifle and left him bleeding to death in the fierce sun. His widow Thelma, 45, said at her home in Whitley Bay on Tyneside: "Douglas died as he had lived, helping others."

In London Iraqi ambassador Azmi Shafiq al-Salihi suggested that the Briton's death was his own fault for trying to cross the border. "The shooting was insignificant compared with killings in Britain," he said. "How many people are murdered in London every night?"

The propaganda war started in earnest. Iraq, which had been trying to jam BBC World Service broadcasts to Kuwait, suddenly offered to pull its 10,000 troops out of the emirate. But Saddam warned that the deal was off if anyone tried to challenge his conquest. His new regime had to stay and the Kuwaiti royal family was banished forever. "Any power, big or small, that intervenes, will have its arm cut off," said Baghdad Radio.

Saddam said he would spell out his demands to Arabs at a summit in the Saudi port of Jeddah. He called on the Emir of Kuwait to face him across the table. But Sheikh Jabar refused to talk to him until his troops pulled out.

In Aspen Mrs Thatcher, branding Saddam an "evil dictator", vowed that there would be no talking until Kuwait was free again. "There is always and there will always be evil in human nature, and we never know where the next threat will come from. The last few days has been evidence of that," she said.

She pressed President Bush to threaten Iraq with military retaliation if Saudi Arabia became the next target. The West began a military build-up. Two British frigates, the Battleaxe and the Jupiter, and two American aircraft carrier groups were ordered to the area.

In the Gulf itself, the threatened states were

maintaining a tactful – some said craven – silence. The press and TV stations, fearful of antagonising Saddam, pretended that the invasion had not happened. It angered their own citizens, who knew full well what was happening from the BBC.

"How can they do that in the late 20th Century when a fellow state has been invaded?" asked one incredulous Dubai resident. "What do they think they are going to achieve?" A United Arab Emirates TV reporter confessed: "I almost cried when we were told not to report the invasion."

It was 36 hours after the invasion that Gulf papers finally carried Saddam's attack on their front pages. There were no leading articles. It was even played down in Saudi Arabia, which had been trying in vain to act as peacemaker.

The United Arab Emirates, not much bigger than Kuwait, had more cause than most to worry. During the Iran-Iraq war they had backed Saddam against Iran's Ayatollah Khomeini. Now Khomeini was dead and Saddam was an even bigger threat. He had been ominously forthright in condemning the Emirates, as well as Kuwait, for busting OPEC's production quotas and undermining his own oil revenues. The Emirates had decided to take a "What's all the fuss about?" approach to the invasion, hoping that Saddam would soften his declared stance towards them. There was fear too in Bahrain, the tiny island state to the north. Foreign journalists attempting to set up base there were refused visas to enter the normally hospitable island.

Kuwaitis at home and abroad felt aggrieved that their Gulf neighbours had failed to condemn the invasion. The only Arab country to swiftly denounce Saddam was Egypt. "This is the blackest day in the history of Arabs," said Cairo's respected al-Ahram paper. "It returns them to the early days of jahilive (the age of barbarism) when the sword ruled and the spilling of blood was the way to solve problems."

Kuwait TV showed pictures of what it claimed were Iraqi armoured divisions going home. But American spy satellites revealed that MORE troops arriving in Kuwait. There was evidence that thousands were digging in along the Saudi border.

President Bush denounced Saddam as a liar and sent Defence Secretary Dick Cheney for talks with the Saudis, who had already deployed 300 tanks along the frontier. The Saudi media, as coy as its neighbours, had not been mentioning Iraq by name but had moved on from calling for the need for Arab brotherhood to condemning the idea of one country occupying another. The country's Okaz newspaper finally summed up the invasion as "an Arab bullet fired from an Arab weapon into the heart of Arab solidarity".

The exiled Kuwaiti Emir appeared on Saudi TV pledging that Kuwait would regain its independence. His ambassador in London announced that 700 Kuwaitis had been killed in the invasion including seven members of the ruling family.

Hundreds of Britons, Germans and Americans

OPEC: OIL KINGDOMS WITH THE WEST AT THEIR FEET

The idea behind the formation of OPEC, the Organisation of Oil Exporting Countries, was simple. The West had too much money and not enough oil. The producers had too much oil and not enough money.

It was in that belief that OPEC began on a sultry autumn day in 1960 in Baghdad.

Gathered together were Iran, Iraq, Kuwait, Saudi Arabia and Venezuela. They were determined to resist the price cuts that Western oil companies were trying to enforce. They were committed to transferring wealth from the West to the Third World.

As they raised the standard against the West they were joined by other producers. Qatar in 1961, Indonesia and Libya a year later and Abu Dhabi in 1967. Algeria joined in 1969, Nigeria in 1971 and Ecuador and Gabon in 1973.

For the first ten years OPEC was content to use its influence to try to prevent falls in oil prices. But by 1970 the cartel had come to realise that it had the industrial world at its mercy. It was determined to ensure it got what it considered a fair price for its products.

OPEC's tactic was the Oil Shock, a huge rise in prices together with a threat to cut off supplies unless the West paid up. In 1973-4, following the Arab-Israeli Yom Kippur war, the price of oil quadrupled.

For the next four years prices stabilised. The industrial nations recovered from the recession caused by the first rise. In 1979 it happened again, with OPEC doubling oil prices.

OPEC had always been more about money than unity, and as each member embarked on ambitious domestic spending programmes each found reasons to exceed their OPEC production quota.

Meanwhile the West found sources from countries outside OPEC. Some major producers, like America and Russia, had never been members, and huge new fields like Alaska and the North Sea further diluted the demand for OPEC oil.

This together with energy-saving measures meant that whilst in 1979 Opec produced more than 66 per cent of the world's petrol, by 1988 the figure was less than 30 per cent.

For some countries, such as Nigeria, this was a disaster. Many of the hardest hit OPEC members blamed countries like Saudi Arabia and Kuwait for over-producing even though they too were exceeding their quotas.

Most were content to complain. But Saddam had a war-ravaged country and needed to rebuild it or fall. When OPEC would not do his bidding and cut production to bring oil up to $25 a barrel, he decided to act.

were being rounded up by troops in Kuwait and bussed to Baghdad, where the population was drilling for mass evacuation in case of Western air raids. The Iraqi line was that the expatriates had been removed for their own safety.

The crisis over the 35 British servicemen being held was played down by embassy staff trying to negotiate their release. Officials were anxious to say or do nothing that might provoke the unpredictable Iraqi dictator. Armed Forces Minister Archie Hamilton surprised some observers by suggesting that Britain had "very good, civilised relations with the Iraqi authorities" and he didn't think that threats would be very useful.

Motorists in Britain were facing a record price of £2.25 for a gallon of petrol, a rise of 10.5p on forecourt prices.

MPs demanded action over the crisis and a recall of Parliament, which was in summer recess. The Tory MP for Selly Oak, Anthony Beaumont-Dark, said it was no excuse to say it was holiday time. "In America, President Bush promised a military blockade of sea, land and air to choke Iraq's war machine.

The stakes were getting higher.

The UN Security Council in New York voted 13 to 0 to impose sanctions and tighten the screw on Iraq. Mrs Thatcher, still in America, said she had never seen the world so united.

She appeared on the steps of the White House with President Bush and NATO's Secretary-General Manfred Woerner in a move to show the world that the West was united in its resolve to deal with the invasion.

Only Yemen and Fidel Castro's Cuba abstained in the UN vote. It was the third time in the UN's 45-year history that the world body had imposed sanctions against a member state. The last time was in 1967 against the white minority government of Rhodesia and an arms embargo against South Africa was still in effect.

The sanctions called for a worldwide ban on oil purchases from Iraq and occupied Kuwait and a stop to all other trade and financial dealings. Food was removed from the list following objections from Ethiopia, a council member with first-hand experience of starvation on a massive scale, because it didn't like the idea that some member states wanted to starve Iraq into submission. Food was to be allowed into Iraq and occupied Kuwait "in humanitarian circumstances". The two countries imported £1,069 million worth of food a year.

There was intense discussion among diplomats over precisely what exports to Iraq were forbidden by the resolution. The consensus appeared to be that grain, beef and animal feeds would be permitted at much lower levels but that luxury items would be forbidden.

Policing the blockade was expected to be a nightmare. But not impossible. As Saudi and Iraqi troops squared up to each other across the fragile frontier, America's aircraft carrier Saratoga and the battleship Wisconsin set sail with 15 other warships and 10,000 men to enforce the UN sanctions.

The fleet would give President Bush 37 warships in striking distance of Iraq within 10 days. A battle force of 15,000 US Marines had already left Virginia for the Eastern Mediterranean and the Royal Navy frigate York, stationed off Dubai, was being joined by other British frigates sailing from Mombasa and Penang. The French were also sending two frigates and there were reports of a Soviet battleship on its way.

US Defence Secretary Dick Cheney was trying to persuade Saudi Arabia's King Fahd to let him use bunkered airbases deep in the desert for 144 warplanes including F1-11 bombers from Britain. There were reports that American B52 bombers had already flown into Egypt to join state-of-the-art Stealth attack craft.

Britain's Aldershot-based 5th Airborne Brigade were on exercise in nearby Oman where they had a permanent base. It was believed that SAS squads, specialists in the desert, had already been despatched to Saudi Arabia where Special Boat Section troops were training alongside members of the American Delta Force, the crack unit trained in hostage rescue.

"The type of people you are talking about are communications experts, logistics men and intelligence specialists," a military source told the Daily Express. "They speak the language and they know the desert. They are there."

Israel issued gas masks to its population when Mossad secret agents revealed that Iraq had moved poison gas shells to the Saudi border, where 120,000 of its troops were now backed by 500 tanks.

Egypt ordered the mobilisation of its army, the Arab world's second largest, which had large numbers of battle-hardened troops and an arsenal of up-to-date US weapons and equipment.

Iraq's chief enemies in the Middle East, Syria and Iran, teamed up to declare their unity against Saddam and his military machine.

Warships from the major sea powers began to converge on the Gulf. They had the ability to cut every sea exit through which Iraq could export the oil that was its economic lifeblood.

Carrier-borne American carrying F-18 Hornet fighters, glamorous F-14 "Top Gun" Tomcat attack fighters and A-6E Intruder bombers would be patrolling the entrance to the Gulf within days. The carriers also had KA-6D tanker jets for the mid-air refuelling of strike aircraft.

They were part of the mightiest armada assembled since the Vietnam or any other war. The aircraft from the US carrier Independence alone could fill four Heathrow hangars. They had a greater combined firepower than that used in World War II. At 80,000 tons the Independence towered above the sea as high as a 22-storey skyscraper and housed 5,500 fighting men. Its flight deck covered 4 acres. The carrier had three stores, three barber shops, a dry-cleaning plant and 2,000 televisions.

"Everybody watches the TV news," said one officer. "We are thirsting for knowledge here. It's two days old but it's still news to us."

The main fear was that Saddam would unleash his fearsome chemical weapons against the fleet, as he had not hesitated to do against his own unarmed villagers in Kurdish northern Iraq.

He had long-range SCUD missiles and several thousand tonnes of chemical weapons including mustard gas. With the help of the West Germans and other Europeans, Saddam had also been manufacturing nerve gas, at a heavily-defended complex 43 miles north-west of Baghdad.

A Pentagon official admitted to the Daily Express: "We have equipment to help our troops

GUARDIAN WOULD BRING PEACE AND SECURITY TO THE MEEK AND DEFENCLESS

Crisis point: The UN Security Council calls for the withdrawal of Iraqi forces from Kuwait hours after the invasion

but fighting a war with heavy protective clothing in that theatre with temperatures around 140F is what we dread for our men."

Like the navy, the US forces taking up positions in Saudi Arabia were equipped with gas masks and gas-proof suits which included overboots, gloves and head cowls.

Mustard gas blisters skin and burns out eyes and lungs. Nerve gas kills in seconds if inhaled and can be fatally absorbed through the suits and skin during prolonged exposure. Its symptoms are diarrhoea, convulsions and such violent vomiting that victims often choke to death.

But the commander of the US naval force, Rear Admiral William Fogerty, said aboard his flagship the USS La Salle: "I feel confident that we are prepared to defend ourselves. The fact that they have chemical weapons is disturbing to everybody but we are a trained force if they happen to employ them."

Another Iraqi weapon which naval commanders feared was the Exocet missile. With its occupation of Kuwait Iraq had captured eight high-speed patrol boats all armed with Exocets, making them a potential threat to the allied ships. The Royal Navy remembered the missiles well from the Falklands war. It was a chilling scenario.

The world tightened its economic stranglehold and Turkey turned off the taps at its end of Iraq's oil pipeline to the Mediterranean. The pipeline carried half of Iraq's oil exports. Its closure and the looming naval blockade left the pipeline through Saudi Arabia as the only artery for Iraqi oil. But the flow had been cut to a trickle as buyers for Iraqi oil shopped elsewhere following the UN embargo.

Then came another body blow for Saddam. Late on Monday evening, August 10, his fellow Moslems turned against him and voted to send their own forces to oppose his vision of conquest.

Saddam had called on the Arab nations to join a jihad a holy war to back his invasion. Allah was on his side, he claimed. But at a stormy summit in Cairo a dozen Arab leaders stood up to him.

The moderate Arab leaders agreed to send

their own peace-making force into Saudi Arabia. They gave Arab League secretary-general Chadli al-Kalibi 15 days to make arrangements for the troops. For Saddam it meant almost total isolation.

He had gone on Iraqi television to announce: "We call you to a holy war. Do not hesitate. Stand up against the outrage of foreign troops in our lands and you will find victory. All believers in God, wherever you are, this is your day to rise up and protest."

A screaming mob in Amman, Jordan, burned American and British flags. A mullah whipped them into a frenzy, crying: "The first enemy that must be eliminated is America the Satan. Either America withdraws or Islam will trample you."

The Cairo Summit put an end to such demonstrations. Middle East giants Egypt and Syria were among the nations in favour of sending Arab troops with only Iraq itself, Libya and the PLO opposing the package of measures.

The Emir of Kuwait had looked a lost and forlorn figure at the summit and his foreign minister collapsed after bitter exchanges with the Iraqi delegation.

Egyptian president Hosni Mubarak said: "The choice in front of us is clear: An Arab act that will preserve higher Arab interests and both Iraq and Kuwait, or a foreign intervention in which we have no say or control. There is no way out except through the withdrawal of Iraqi troops from Kuwait."

Saddam offered a peace deal. He said he would negotiate in return for an end to economic sanctions, a pull-out of all non-Arab troops from Saudi Arabia, an Arab force to replace them under the UN flag without Egyptian participation and the withdrawal of Israel from its occupied territories.

His plan was promptly dismissed by Downing Street and the White House. But one of President Bush's advisers said: "His offer to negotiate is the first sign of his willingness to move away from hostilities. We are still eyeball-to-eyeball, but at least he has just blinked."

GERM WARFARE: ONLY A STIFLING SUIT OFFERED SURVIVAL

Chemical weapons have been described as the poor man's atom bomb, but the comparison is a false one. A nuclear weapon will destroy any men, arms or defences within the target area. Chemical or biological agents can injure only unprotected troops.

Most chemical weapons are "binary" a combination of two or more chemicals which are harmless in themselves but deadly when combined.

As well as germ warfare weapons like anthrax and cholera warheads, Iraq has blister agents such as mustard gas,

semi-permanent nerve gases such as Sarin and Soman, poison gases like cyanide and the long-lasting nerve gas VX.

All of these can be delivered by short or long range artillery, as Iraq did during the Gulf War with Iran, by missile or by one of Iraq's ten Soviet SU24 Fencer bombers.

Saddam has already used air-dropped nerve gas on the rebellious Kurds of northern Iraq but the sophisticated NBC (Nuclear, Biological, Chemical) suits and training of the Allies give them a chance of survival not available to the 5,000 unprotected Kurdish people.

Saddam made the offer in a speech on Iraqi television and radio. He called for his initiative to be considered alongside other Middle East problems. The UN could decide on the size and deployment of the Arab force in Saudi Arabia, he said, But only Iraq and Saudi Arabia would select the countries making up the force.

The offer was doomed to failure as soon as Israeli leaders dismissed any suggestion that they would give up their occupied territories. But at the time the conciliatory nature of Saddam's speech was seen by many diplomats as a sign that the Iraqi leader realised he was in an impossible position. With American forces arriving by the hour in Saudi Arabia and Arab troops joining them even as he spoke, Saddam was beginning to realise that the odds were stacked against him, they argued. It was still early days.

In a plea to Iraq's women Saddam warned for the first time of the consequences of defeat. He said the Arabs would be thrown into disarray and poverty at the hands of the Americans and Jews. The women and children of Iraq would have to make sacrifices to survive.

Food rationing was to be introduced and people found hoarding would be sentenced to death. "Every family in Iraq can live without buying clothes for one year," said Saddam. "Everyone should behave in a way to halve their usual food consumption and change their diets." By sacrificing themselves they had the promise of "massive wealth and a better future after victory".

"By doing this we can strike the American plans in the heart," he said. "They think that money and food is everything in life." Baghdad Radio played patriotic songs.

More than 4,000 American troops from the 82nd Airborne Division were already protecting F16 and F15 jets at airbases in the Saudi desert as a huge air and sea lift of troops, weapons and ammunition from Britain and the US got under way. A dozen RAF Tornado jets landed in Saudi Arabia, and tank-busting Jaguar strike aircraft flew in to Oman.

But back home some leaders of Britain's 1.5 million Moslems denounced the Gulf task force and demanded that it return home. In an impassioned statement representatives of 35 Moslem groups cited the Koran and said: "We cannot tolerate the intervention of non-Moslem powers in this affair."

The statement, read by Yusef Islam the former pop singer Cat Stevens said current borders dividing the Moslem states were artificial divisions imposed by former colonial powers.

"The build-up of non-Moslem forces in the vicinity of Islam's most holy shrines of Mecca,

Medina and Jerusalem is not acceptable," he said.

Tory MPs Humfrey Malins and Sir Bernard Braine said Moslems had a duty to back Britain.

Sher Azam, president of the Bradford Council for Mosques, responded: "It should have been left to the Arab world to resolve this issue."

But the Arab world had voted for sanctions and to ally itself militarily with the West. The whole world was united against Saddam. Men and arms were assembling in the Gulf.

It was, in Churchill's phrase, the end of the beginning.

Flashpoint: Pro-Iraqi demonstrators burn the Union Jack in Jordan

CHAPTER 2

THE GULF WAR

As August drew to a close television viewers were treated to a propaganda stunt of unprecedented cynicism. Saddam put aside his uniform and dressed in a smart suit for the cameras, surrounded himself with children and played Mr Nice Guy.

In a 40-minute screen appearance he patted his young hostages on the heads and told them: "You are the heroes of peace."

The children flinched and turned away as he tried to play the father figure. Eleven-year-old Ian Morton, from Middlesbrough, looked terrified as Saddam reached out and tried to stroke Stuart Lockwood, five, who folded his arms and refused to be won over by the dictators avuncular approach.

His defiance, as Saddam held his arm, moved the world.

"Are you getting your milk? Ah, with cornflakes too. That's good," the dictator said to him through an interpreter.

The children's parents looked bemused to find themselves confronted by their captor trying to be nice.

"Please forgive us because like Stuart and Ian, we have our own children and our own families and we know how you feel. But we are trying to stop a war," Saddam told them. "Your presence here is meant to prevent the scourge of battle."

He asked Stuart, from Worcester, if he had any brothers or sisters. "A 14-year-old brother," the boy's father, engineer Derek Lockwood, replied.

Saddam then told all the hostages: "I am sure

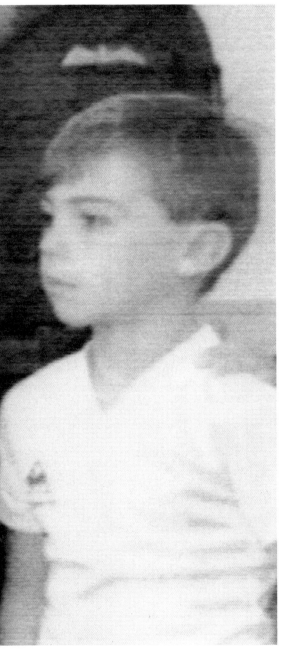

'You are dealing with a tyrant who has played out a callous charade on TV with children and yet has not hesitated to use chemical weapons against the innocent young of his country'

Margaret Thatcher

Tragedy in the hills. A Kurdish mother and her baby, victims of Saddam's germ warfare attack Left: Saddam holds Stuart Lockwood in a TV appearance that shocked the West

Stuart will be happy to have as part of his personal history the fact that he played a role in maintaining peace."

Time and again he assured the 20 captives that they were "guests" of Iraq. Apparently quite relaxed, with one arm on his knee, he said: "As Iraqis, Arabs and human beings we want you to be safe. You are not hostages. We would have liked to get to know you in other circumstances. We hope your presence here is not going to be long."

Pointing to one of the children, he added: "When he, along with his friends and all those present here have played their role in preventing war, then they will all be heroes of peace."

Saddam was flanked by Iraqi air force chiefs as he addressed the group, who sat on settees and chairs in the white-walled room. One of his aides took notes. The atmosphere tensed as he blamed Britain and America for the Gulf crisis and revealed there had been no fresh negotiation for the hostages' release.

"We do not want war to come about, despite the fact that we know we can smash and crush the opposition," he said. "The question that has to be posed by all of us to Mrs Thatcher and Mr Bush is, What has Iraq taken away from them which has made them bring their armies to the region and to threaten its people?"

Explaining his invasion of Kuwait he said: "How would you feel if part of England was cut away from your country? Wouldn't you find that harmful? I am sure you would deplore this. It is the same thing for Iraqis."

Saddam said he was prepared to answer any questions and told one mother who was cradling a baby in her arms that teachers would be brought in for the youngsters. "We will make sure the children are not deprived," he said.

And beaming at the children, he claimed that God would help him find a way out of the crisis.

The hostages, though obviously ill-at-ease, were determined not to show any fear as Saddam warned that he would not be blackmailed. Iraq would stand firm and destroy any aggressors.

"They will fail and they will find that world public opinion will turn against them even inside England and the US," he said.

Bringing the performance to a conclusion he grouped the hostages together for a photograph with him. "We will ensure your messages reach your families in England. As of now, you can write your messages and letters and you can take photographs if you want," he told them.

Mrs Thatcher, watching in London, said the spectacle filled her with revulsion. "This is quite sickening," she told officials. "If he wants to be nice to children the simplest way is to let them go."

Washington denounced Saddam's "shameful theatrics" and Foreign Secretary Douglas Hurd said: "Here is a man completely unscrupulous in his choice of means." Iraq's policy of seizing a human shield of hostages was evil and useless, he added.

Relatives of the captives, watching at home, had looked on aghast as Saddam toyed with the loved ones they feared would disappear forever.

It had been a momentous week.

A plan by Saddam to round up Britons and Americans in Kuwait had turned into a shambles. He had ordered 4,000 UK passport holders, women and children included, to report to the Regency Palace Hotel in Kuwait City "for their own safety." Britons obeying his command turned up at the hotel to find no Iraqis to shepherd them. They took the advice of a British diplomat on duty in the reception area and left. US citizens had already been told not to comply with the instruction.

Saddam had threatened that anyone ignoring the order would face "unspecified difficulties". There were fears in Whitehall that Britons rounded up would be sent to Iraq and herded into detention camps. Douglas Hurd flew back to London from Italy to take charges of Britain's response to the dictator's latest move. Foreign Minister William Waldegrave denounced Saddam's order as a "grave and sinister development".

"It is a further example of the duplicity of the Iraqi regime," he said. "We fear that Britons will be interned somewhere else, most likely Iraq."

Mrs Thatcher, on holiday in Cornwall, telephoned Kuwait's deputy prime minister, Sheikh Sabah Ahmed al-Sabah, to reassure him that Britain was standing firm on demands for Saddam's invasion force to withdraw. And Italy's representative at the UN called for an emissary to be sent to Baghdad to secure the release of all foreigners.

Saddam offered a deal to Iran. Nearly two years after his ceasefire with the Ayatollahs he announced a startling and complete capitulation to Teheran's peace demands. He promised to withdraw 400,000 troops from Iranian territory and exchange prisoners of war. And he abandoned his battle for control of the Shatt al-Arab waterway, the territorial dispute that had triggered the countries' bloody eight-year fight.

The move was believed to be part of a comprehensive "peace initiative" contained in a letter from Saddam which would-be mediator, King Hussein of Jordan, took to Mr Bush's holiday home in Maine.

The King was America's favourite Arab leader. He felt that only a negotiated Arab solution would save his own throne and America from a catastrophic war. But The White House knew that the King's plan involved the survival of Saddam and some kind of Iraqi control of Kuwait.

Safe Haven? Kuwait's luxury Regency Palace Hotel. Britons were ordered to report there ...but no Iraqis turned up

President Bush, to show his anger at the Iraqi dictator, kept the royal peacemaker waiting for a day before seeing him then rejected his proposals.

It was obvious to the West that the deal with Iran would allow Saddam to reinforce his huge garrison facing the Saudi and American forces. And Iraq would gain hand somely from a prisoner exchange Iran held 70,000 Iraqis to Iraq's 30,000 Iranians. The control of the Shatt al-Arab was no longer strategically important to Iraq as long as it could hang onto Kuwait and its better access to Gulf shipping lanes.

But for Saddam a much bigger prize was attainable. To forge a pact with Teheran would unite the Gulf's leading Islamic powers in opposition to America and Britain, who had "invaded" Saudi Arabia and its holy places. The reward would be total control of the Gulf and the OPEC oil cartel. Should that gamble succeed, the military and political power balance confronting the West would shift dramatically.

Days later, however, as Iraq withdrew troops from Iranian territory, Teheran condemned Saddam's invasion of Kuwait and backed UN sanctions against Baghdad. Saddam's stance hardened.

In an ultimatum to the White House he warned that detained foreigners would be freed only if the US withdrew its troops from Saudi Arabia and ended the trade embargo against his country. Otherwise the hostages would be used to deter the growing threat of air strikes against Iraq. Reports reached London of Britons being transported to strategic military bases and oilfields.

Saddam announced that any pre-emptive strike by the U.S. would mean tens of thousands of dead on both sides. "Many of our children and your children will be orphaned if war breaks out and many of your women and our women will become widows," he said in a TV statement. "Our people are seeking to avert a catastrophe. The presence of the foreigners with Iraqi families at vital targets might prevent an attack."

Britain's ambassador to the UN, Sir Crispin Ticekell, said: "I can hardly think of a more outrageous act that any of us in any generation have seen than that which is now taking place at the hands of the Iraqi government."

And for the first time President Bush publicly admitted that Americans detained in the Gulf were hostages. "When Saddam Hussein specifically offers to trade the freedom of those citizens he holds against their will, there can be little doubt that whatever these innocent people are called they are in fact hostages," he said.

He chose a sunny afternoon in Baltimore to give his most sombre warning yet to Americans over the crisis: Be prepared for sacrifice.

"We are engaged in a cause larger than our selves," he told 2,000 war veterans. He compared the threat posed to the world by Saddam as equal to that of Adolf Hitler and promised: "America stands where it has always stood against those who would replace the rule of law."

President Bush quoted General Eisenhower's call on the eve of the D-Day Normandy invasion: "We ask for God's blessing on this great and mighty undertaking."

And thumping the lectern he warned: "I want there to be no misunderstanding. I will hold the government of Iraq responsible for the safety and well-being of American citizens held against their will."

America would not be intimidated, he pledged. But the nation faced a crisis that would require planning, patience and personal sacrifice. "It is a sacrifice we must and will meet if we are to stop aggression, help our friends and defend our own interests in the peace and stability of countries around the globe."

The President said he would not abandon his four conditions for a peaceful settlement in the Gulf. They were:

● The Complete, immediate and unconditional withdrawal of Iraqi forces from Kuwait.
● The Restoration of Kuwait's legitimate government.
● The Security and sovereignty of Saudi Arabia and peace in the Gulf.
● The Safety and protection of American citizens abroad.

"Today these objectives are, and will remain, unchanged," he said. "Will it take time? Of course. For we are engaged in a cause larger than ourselves."

Half a century ago, President Bush said, the world had missed the chance to stop a ruthless aggressor. "I pledge to you we will not make that mistake again."

He recalled America's role during World War II and the battles of Korea and Vietnam.

"One should not under estimate those that threaten peace. But an even greater mistake would be to underestimate our commitment to our friends when our friends are in peril, or our commitment to international order when that too is in peril."

President Bush had decided to send US forces to the Middle East "reluctantly but decisively". Iraq, he said, was guilty of a ruthless assault on "the essence of international order and civilised ideals". His message to Saddam was: "Release all for eigners now. Give them the right to come and go as they wish."

'I will hold the Government of Iraq responsible for the safety and well-being of American citizens held against their will' *George Bush*

'The invasion
is treachery
and a
flagrant
violation of
international
law' *Mikhail Gorbachev*

The veterans cheered him.

The decision to use the term hostages strengthened the basis under international law for US military intervention in the Gulf. Mr Bush had broad legal powers either to retaliate or mount a rescue mission, since international law forbade deliberately using foreigners as human shields at military installations or the holding of hostages.

Shortly after President Bush finished his speech America called for emergency UN Security Council talks to approve Western action. As more countries pledged troops and arms for the Gulf Britain's new commander of the Armilla Patrol in the area, Commodore Paul Haddocks, 43, joined his fleet of 11 ships.

Mr Bush's words brought an immediate response from the Iraqis. "Our foreign guests have been moved to all vital and military installations," a government spokesman said in Baghdad. "They have been provided with all modern facilities and they are in good physical condition."

President Bush had accused Iraqi troops of widespread atrocities in Kuwait. He claimed that the latest intelligence reports showed "a sordid tale of brutality".

In fact efforts were being made by Baghdad to stop looting in Kuwait. An Iraqi officer was left hanging from a crane after being executed for stealing. His booty clothes, television sets and other electrical goods were displayed beneath the body.

"Saddam has claimed that this is a holy war against the infidel," said President Bush. "This from a man who has used poison gas against the men, women and children of his own country, who invaded Iran in a war that cost the lives of half a million Moslems, and who now plunders Kuwait."

The Pentagon, meanwhile, had some disturbing news for the President. The generals warned that a Gulf war would cost America $540 million a day. The White House had no option but to press Saudi Arabia, Japan, West Germany and even Kuwait's exiled government to help foot the bill. It would take $250 million a month just to maintain the US ground, naval and air forces confronting Iraq.

It was a huge undertaking. The last-minute shopping for US paratroops alone included 5,500 tins of foot powder, 4,000 tubes of lip balm, 10,000 bottles of suntan lotion and 174,000 gallons of bottled spring water. Never mind the ammunition.

In the desert, the American troops faced a time-honoured propaganda ploy. Iraq was transmitting English language broadcasts announcing that GIs would be "swallowed by the sand dunes while their women back home enjoyed themselves with rich Arabs".

As Jordan's King Hussein desperately continued to try to find a solution to the crisis, Soviet President Mikhail Gorbachev warned that Iraq had started a "perilous chain reaction" which could engulf the world in war. The Soviet leader condemned Saddam's invasion as "treachery and a blatant violation of international law".

It was the fiercest Russian denunciation yet of the Iraq leader, the man Moscow had once seen as its closest ally in the Middle East. Gorbachev, holidaying on the Black Sea, explained to Russian army units on exercise in Odessa: "We agreed to sell Iraq weapons only to maintain its defence capability."

His foreign minister Eduard Shevardnadze pledged that Russian troops would back any call for a UN multinational force to solve the crisis. The USSR, increasingly worried about the fate of 8,000 Russians in Iraq, had sent four warships to the Gulf. But the Kremlin repeatedly rejected invitations to join the West's task force.

Throughout the Gulf the threat of war had given oil-rich sheikhs the jitters. They were flying out their prized possessions and luxury cars. Lamborghinis were arriving in England to join Aston Martins, Porsches and stretched Mercedes limousines at garages up and down the country.

Saddam's Cadillac was also receiving special treatment. He had shipped it to America for an overhaul before the invasion and President Bush impounded it.

The war of words raged on. Saddam ordered Western diplomats to leave their embassies in Kuwait and report to Baghdad by Friday August 24. Keeping the embassies open would be regarded as an act of aggression, he said. Britain immediately announced that it would defy the

Spoils of war: Saddam's impounded luxury Cadillac, in America for an overhaul

Friends and neighbours: Saddam greets King Hussein of Jordan

demand and Ambassador Michael Weston's 10-man mission refused to budge, pledging to stand by the 4,000 Britons trapped in Kuwait. American, Japanese and other foreign envoys also vowed to stay put.

"We will ensure that Britain has people in Kuwait able to keep in touch with our community for as long as is physically possible," said Douglas Hurd in London. Diplomats would not leave except under force.

Asked whether military muscle would be used to remove the envoys, Iraqi information director Naji al-Hadithi said: "All of them will go but there will be no need for force. Will a diplomat fight with his pencil?"

On the evening of the deadline 53-year-old Mr Weston displayed the bulldog spirit. As Iraqi tanks massed on the front lawn of the embassy and troops cut off the electricity and water supplies, he opened up the cellars and sipped champagne by candlelight with his staff.

Iraqi troops surrounded seven other Western embassies, including America's, and cut the phone lines. No one was allowed in or out. The invaders threatened that all male diplomats would be stripped of their diplomatic status and held hostage if the embassies were not shut down. But families were allowed to leave.

Inside the British Embassy Mr Weston, his consul Larry Banks, first secretary Donald Macauley and security officer Brian McKeith had stocked up with food and supplies. They were determined to keep the Union Flag flying over the sand-coloured building and prepared to destroy vital codes and communication equipment.

Mr Hurd accused the Iraqis of acting illegally, and praised the courage of the ambassador and his staff. "I am grateful to Michael Weston and his three colleagues for their willingness to remain, despite personal risk to themselves," he said. "Iraqi citizens will be held personally responsible, in accordance with international law, for any illegal actions concerning the security and lives of foreign persons."

As tension rose King Hussein, torn between long-standing support for Iraq and friendship with the West, said the world had "gone mad". He announced that he would visit Iraq and other countries in a last-ditch attempt to mediate. Jordan then closed its border with Iraq, cutting off the one remaining chance of escape for many foreigners.

In Kuwait City it had become a game of cat-and-mouse. Iraqi troops were rounding up men and their families at gunpoint.

Some Britons were using an early-warning whistling system. When soldiers approached, the shrills could be heard from one street to the next, giving fugitives enough time to reach the safety of basements, holes behind partition walls and water towers. Those who weren't so quick faced the prospect of being taken to hostels, warehouses if they were luckier, hotels in Baghdad.

One Kuwaiti resistance fighter claimed that a

Briton was forced to watch as Iraqi troops gunned down the family of the man who had sheltered him. Pleas to the soldiers to spare them were answered by a burst of machine gun fire which killed the wife and her five children, according to Yaquob Al-Shatti, a former PR director of Kuwait's exclusive Messilah Beach Hotel. The Briton, an oil company manager, was hauled off to Baghdad with his Kuwaiti helper.

Yaquob also described how a bus he was using to help Westerners to flee was strafed by a Iraqi helicopter gunship. He crouched under the vehicle with a couple from Manchester as machine gun bullets thudded into it. They had heard the helicopter approaching and stopped the bus, burying its wheels in the soft sand to make it appear as if the vehicle had broken down and been abandoned.

Yaqoub, 45, claimed that more than 100 resistance fighters equipped by CIA were making nightly raids over the border from Saudi Arabia. His group had carried out 20 missions bringing more than 100 people to safety through Iraqi lines.

Saddam warned that the treatment of hostages would depend on their government's degree of hostility to Iraq. A Baghdad government spokesman announced: "The accommodation will be varied. The least favourable will be allocated to our guests according to the aggression of the nation concerned."

That could mean no air-conditioning and limited sanitation in a country where summer temperatures reached 120F.

"Food will be rationed in proportion to the amount of stocks available to the people of Iraq,"

the spokesman added.

Hostages were warned of a "final, irrevocable" announcement. Expatriates were ordered to report to assembly points where they would be escorted by troops to their new accommodation. Those failing to obey the decree would be rounded up and allocated inferior quarters on tented sites at military installations most at risk from Western attack. Disobedience would no longer be tolerated by the Iraqi president. There were reports that six giant warehouses were in the final stages of conversion to dormitories where the hostages would be housed under guard.

The round-up would not affect people from other Arab countries, or Turkey, or France, which Saddam saw as a potential maverick at the UN. Austria's president Kurt Waldheim did a deal with Saddam which allowed the ex-Nazi officer to fly home with 100 of his citizens.

In Downing Street the lights burned into the night as Mrs Thatcher held a telephone council of war with President Bush and other world leaders. Both the British and Americans were determined to ensure that sanctions against Iraq were effective. The Royal Navy was now ready to disable any ships breaching the economic embargo.

One of the British warships policing the Gulf was the 3,000-ton HMS Jupiter. Expressman Norman Luck joined the frigate and reported:

"In a simulated Action Stations alert I learned that the distance from my bunk to the gundeck was a staggering 33 steep steps, four narrow hatches, two ladders and a bruise on the head for bobbing up when I should have stooped...to be completed in 90 seconds.

Saddam the warrior: The Iraqi leader eyes the Saudi border from a bunker in Kuwait

SADDAM: MAN WITH A VISION AND A TASTE FOR WHISKY WH

"I failed. But the rest of the ship's company did not. They have had far more practice than I, and were spurred on by the fact that they would get chips for dinner.

"Chips are a rare commodity in the Gulf because no deep-fat fryers can be used on board. The last thing Commander John Wright wants in the confusion of Action Stations is chip pans flying and hot fat splashing around the ship.

"Above decks many of the crew remain on station checking and rechecking guns, hosing down the Exocets with sea water to stop them cooking, and joking with the Royal Marines drafted in to join the operation.

"The bridge is cool and air-conditioned. In the "eyes" of the ship, a team of officers and men peers monotonously into the heat haze across the green sea for unidentified merchant shipping trying to break the sanctions embargo.

"Battle bags hanging from the bulkheads, containing chemical and bacterial warfare suits, anti-flash gear, gas-masks and overalls are a constant reminder that danger lurks at the push of a button. I sat down to dinner in the Officers' Mess but lost my appetite when told that the table we were sitting at was the emergency operating table in times of combat."

And combat was looking more likely. Mrs Thatcher warned the world that a negotiated settlement with Iraq was unlikely.

"The United Nations has ruled that Saddam must totally withdraw from Kuwait and the legitimate government be restored," she said. "I doubt very much whether he will do that.

"There will be no negotiations with a man who takes over, by force, someone else's country. You are dealing with a dictator who is an absolute tyrant, who has played out a callous charade on TV with children and yet has not hesitated to use chemical weapons against the innocent young of his country. This man is a despot and a tyrant and must be stopped."

As Mrs Thatcher prepared to meet King Hussein, Saddam warned: "We want peace. But if the United States attacks there will be a column of dead bodies which may have a beginning but will have no end."

aghdad staged another TV propaganda stunt. The occasion was the white wedding of Britons Debbie Hayes and Leslie Roberts.

The ceremony, screened to millions of Iraqis, began with the announcer saying: "We are showing this wedding in the hope the hysteria of the Bush administration will be calmed."

It opened with shots of a terrace bedecked with flowers. Two pretty young Iraqi girls walked towards the camera holding lighted candles. A four-piece string quartet played the Wedding March as the bride, wearing a full-length white dress and veil, appeared.

An Anglian priest conducted the service and when he said: "You may kiss the bride," there were whoops of joy from the guests. The film went on to show the wedding buffet with the couple cutting a three-tier cake and guests toasting them with champagne and dancing.

The priest said: "It has been a glittering occasion and we are overwhelmed by the friendship and kindness of the Iraqis."

Sales executive Debbie, 24, added: "We wanted

BUILT THE HANGING GARDENS OF BABYLON IN HIS NAME

He picked up a gun for the first time at 10 and some say he killed his first man at 19. Saddam Hussein saw himself as a man of destiny whose task it was to reunite the Arab world or die trying.

Saddam al-Takriti was born in 1937 to a peasant household in Takrit, north of Baghdad. His father died when the boy was a child and he was adopted by his uncle, an army officer who often beat him.

Saddam's school career was undistinguished. He failed in his one ambition when he was rejected by the Military Academy at the age of 16. This pushed him into political activism and he joined the illegal Ba'ath Party, a Right-wing organisation with visions of Arab unity.

Later Saddam was forced to flee to Egypt. It was there that he married his wife of 30 years, his cousin Sagida. She bore him three daughters and two sons.

Returning to Iraq he took part in the Ba'ath coup of 1968. In July 1979 he seized power. Only one man's word was law in Iraq. "A law is a piece of paper on which we write one or two lines and then sign it Saddam Hussein," he said.

Saddam altered the past as well as the future. He changed his ancestry to trace descent from King Nebuchadnezzar, the builder of Babylon who enslaved the Jews, and from the Prophet Mohammed.

His quest to re-establish a Golden Age in Iraq led him to rebuild the Hanging Gardens of Babylon on their original site. When Nebuchadnezzar built the Gardens every 10th brick bore the message "Built in the time of Nebuchadnezzar". This time every fourth brick read "Built in the time of Saddam."

Like many who were born into poverty, Saddam loved the good things in life. His favourite drink was Johnny Walker Black Label whisky. And as befitted a man who never spent more than one night at a time anywhere, because of any assassination attempt, Saddam had a series of sumptuous palaces and a luxurious bunker under one of his mansions in Baghdad, with an underground tunnel linking it to an airstrip.

Kurdish leader Jalal Talabani summed him up: "Whenever I went to see Saddam I expected he would either empty his revolver into my head or make me a present of it. Both reactions would have been calculated in advance."

a simple wedding in jeans. Instead there was a cake, a dress and even a children's choir. The Iraqis have been fantastic to us. This is a night we will always remember."

Leslie said: "We are delighted to be here. I cannot thank the Iraqis enough."

In the circumstances they could not have been expected to say anything else. But later a letter from Debbie to her parents in Beverley, Humberside, was smuggled out.

Writing postcard-style, Debbie said: "The situation in Kuwait very disturbing. Many of my friends killed, we are under house arrest with guards outside each floor. I am OK and I must keep others happy as people are doing for me. Be on your knees for the things you have. Never complain because you don't know how lucky you are."

The strain on the relatives and loved ones of the hostages was enormous. The helplessness of their situation was highlighted by 20-year-old nurse Kirrin Robinson, who wrote to the Daily Express telling of her anguish.

Her father, electrical engineer Robert, had left his home in Keighley, West Yorkshire, for Kuwait a fortnight before the invasion. Kirrin wrote:

"My Dad, Robert Robinson, is a hostage in Kuwait. I have no idea whether he is alive or dead or if I will ever see him again. I am expected to carry on my life whilst he is a pawn in a political game of chess.

"No one seems to care. I live from day to day listening to every news broadcast, the only link with what is happening in Kuwait. Every time the phone rings I dread to answer in case it is news of his death.

"What I don't understand is why my family is in this position. Is oil so valuable that it far outweighs human life?

"I have a feeling of helplessness, an inability to look beyond the next news bulletin.

"As a nurse, I spend my days caring for people, yet no-one seems to care what happens to my Dad. Why? For oil!

"This should have been a happy time for the family with my 21st birthday and planning for my sister's wedding. How can we celebrate without my Dad being there? I realise I am one of many in this position, but Robert Robinson is my Dad and that makes him special."

Kirrin sent an identical message to Mrs Thatcher.

But there was good news on the hostage front to balance at least some of the bad. Another freedom convoy of Britons arrived safely in Saudi Arabia led by Bedouin tribesmen.

Nine vehicles with 30 people on board had driven at 75mph through a barrage of bullets to reach the border in four hours. As they arrived in their bullet-riddled cars businessman Tony Stevens, 38 from Southampton, said: "We decided to risk the trip because we did not want to be held as hostages.

"Thank God for the Bedouin tribesmen. They guided us. One of them took the wheel of the leading vehicle and off we went. We put our trust in them. We know they had already made 16 escape runs to ferry others to safety and they would take no payment.

"It was the most frightening, and amazing, drive of my life. We were hitting over 75mph the whole way but these guys knew what were they doing. Iraqi troops kept firing at us and bullets were zinging by, but we could not see where they were coming from.

"We fell to the floor and our Bedouin driver was incredible. Whenever the Iraqis started shooting he clapped his hands in delight, turned up the music and started singing loudly.

"We had the windows wide open and the sound of Arab music must have carried through the desert. If the Iraqis could not see us they certainly must have heard us.

"In Kuwait City Mubarak Hospital is stacked with bodies of people who have made a bid for freedom and failed. Many are unidentified. Some died from dehydration, others are riddled with bullets."

Then came some really good news. Saddam agreed to release all the women and children he was holding.

The breakthrough came after he met a group of Western parents and their children in Baghdad. One brave mother asked him: "Why are you using our children as pawns?"

Later, an announcement on Iraqi TV claimed that Saddam had been deeply affected by their appeals to be allowed to go home. He had decided the women and children would enjoy "the freedom of staying or leaving". The TV statement said the decision was made "to preserve the image of Arabs".

The move was followed by a scurry of diplomatic activity. British embassy officials in Amman prepared a mass evacuation plan.

Saddam patted himself on the back by renaming Kuwait in his honour. He announced that the "province" would be called Saddamiyat Al-Mitlaa and Kuwait City would be known as Kadhima. The new title put back the clock hundreds of years to the Ottoman Empire when Kuwait, as Kadhima, was a busy trading port at the head of the Gulf.

But now it was busy no more. It was a dead city, occupied by foreign troops and haunted by fear. No change of name could alter that.

CHAPTER

3

THE GULF

WAR

'It's not the size of the dog in the fight, it's the size of the fight in the dog.'

General Norman Schwarzkopf

While Kuwait suffered, the wheels of war were turning. In a second-floor office in the Pentagon the highest-ranking soldier in America was quietly fine-tuning the world's mightiest military machine.

General Colin Powell's job was to orchestrate Operation Desert Shield. There were 70,000 servicemen and women in Saudi Arabia with more arriving hourly. Thousands of tons of equipment, from tanks to paper cups, were being shipped in. One US company had been asked to supply a million cans of foot powder. Another received orders for 240,000lbs of frozen chickens. Supplies equivalent to half a million tons of Chevrolet vehicles had been shifted.

General Powell, son of a seamstress in the slums of Harlem, had been burning the midnight oil in company with many of the Pentagon's 23,000 military personnel. His day started at 4am. He went home at 8pm and worked on in his study, linked to the Pentagon and the White

General Colin Powell, the most powerful military man in the world. His day started at 4am…and never ended.

House by a secure and secret communications system.

Next to his office in the Pentagon was the Crisis Action Team, or CAT. The team consisted of 40 people who worked 12-hour shifts in a simple room monitoring developments and helping to formulate US response to events in the Gulf. The pace was hectic and the air was laden with the aromas of microwaved popcorn and takeaway pizzas.

General Powell's man in the Middle East was General Norman Schwarzkopf, Commander in Chief of the United States Central Command, CENTCOM. Stormin' Norman or The Bear, as he was nicknamed because of his burly 6ft3ins frame first heard of the Iraqi invasion of Kuwait as it happened when the phone rang at his home on the MacDill airbase in Florida.

On the line was Powell, who told him that the Iraqis had just crossed the border. Schwarzkopf, who had just changed into a tracksuit for a workout, rushed straight to his command centre without changing back into uniform. Days later he flew to Saudi Arabia and established Command Control in Riyadh, the capital. He was later to impress the Allies with some tough words on the Iraqis: 'It's not the size of the dog in the fight. It's the size of the fight in the dog!'

President Bush had made a special request to NATO for ships capable of carrying thousands of troops, tanks and supplies to the Gulf. Britain and Italy immediately agreed to the request and roll-on roll-off car ferries were put on standby.

And every 15 minutes around the clock a US warplane was rolling down the runway at Scott Airforce base, 20 miles from St Louis, en route for the Middle East.

The fat bellies of the giant Galaxy and Starlifter transports were filled to the ribs with the Pentagon's war equipment. There were more than 200 transports in the air at any one time and it was possible to watch them all at once, crossing three continents and thousands of miles of ocean, on a giant wall-to-wall computer screen deep inside the red-brick building housing MAC, America's Military Airlift Command.

Sunday Express journalist Rowena Webster was the first British reporter allowed inside the nerve centre of Operation Desert Shield. She wrote:

"MAC, under the command of Colonel Darryl Bottjer, has not closed its watchful eye since the invasion of Kuwait. Within minutes of the Iraqi tanks crossing the border Bottjer's Crisis Action Team was roused from its sleep and has hardly rested since.

"Just a few years ago Bottjer and his team would have been moving wooden airplanes along magnetic wall maps. Today their ops room is of Star Trek specifications. Giant monitors project complex computer-generated maps and graphics on the walls in front of them. Every plane flying a sortie for Desert Shield is represented and colour-coded C5 Galaxy transports in red, C-141 Starlifters in blue.

"Any part of the world can be picked out and magnified on screen to scrutinise aircraft movements there in greater detail. Next to each giant screen fluorescent green and orange signs flash up world time differences. At 11.46am at Scott Air Force Base it is already 7.46pm in Saudi Arabia.

POWELL: WORLD WATCHES TOUGH GUY FROM THE BRONX

The destiny of America's troops in the Gulf rested in the hands of 53-year-old General Colin Powell, chairman of the Joint Chiefs of Staff and the most powerful military man in the US.

He was born in 1937, the son of poor Jamaicans who had sought a new life in New York during the early 1920s. His father Luther was a shipping clerk and his mother Maud a seamstress.

He was brought up with his sister Marilyn in the tough and teeming Bronx. The young Colin learnt Yiddish a talent that astonished many unsuspecting Jews discussing the schwarze in his presence.

He also learned from his devoutly Christian parents the values that inspired him to rise to the top, values that led many to believe he could be the first black President.

Colin Luther Powell grew up into a handsome young man, 6ft 2ins tall and weighing 14 stone. He graduated from New York's City College with a degree in geology in 1958.

He immediately joined the army as a lowly 2nd Lieutenant and served two tours of duty in Vietnam, being wounded twice and winning the Purple Heart and the Bronze Star for rescuing comrades from a blazing helicopter.

The turning point in his career came when he was 35. Powell was chosen from 1,500 applicants as one of 17 White House Fellows, a programme designed to introduce fresh talent into Washington.

By luck he was posted to the Office of Management and Budget, a department run by Caspar Weinberger, later Defence Secretary to Ronald Reagan, and Frank Carlucci, later his National Security Adviser.

With their patronage he rose rapidly through the ranks, becoming Weinberger's senior assistant and succeeding Carlucci as National Security Adviser.

The pinnacle of his career came in 1989 when George Bush picked him over the heads of 30 more senior generals to chair the Joint Chiefs of Staff.

For all his meteoric rise to the top of America's establishment Powell retained his common touch, spending as much time as he could at home with his wife Alma and their three children and indulging in his hobby of restoring, of all things, derelict Volvos.

Only in America could a black, Yiddish-speaking amateur mechanic become the most powerful soldier in the country.

OPERATION DESERT SHIELD

Above: The Marines arrive in Saudi.
Below: Their awesome rocket firepower.

Sky Heroes: Phantom pilots used their missiles to destroy enemy ground radar

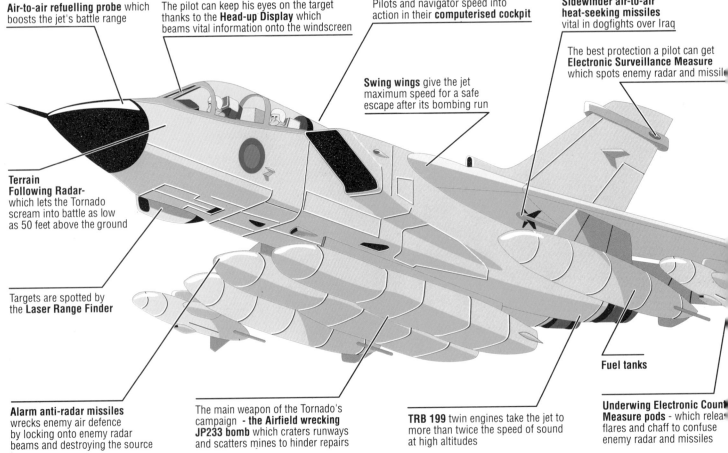

Air-to-air refuelling probe which boosts the jet's battle range

The pilot can keep his eyes on the target thanks to the **Head-up Display** which beams vital information onto the windscreen

Pilots and navigator speed into action in their **computerised cockpit**

Sidewinder air-to-air heat-seeking missiles vital in dogfights over Iraq

The best protection a pilot can get **Electronic Surveillance Measure** which spots enemy radar and missile

Terrain Following Radar- which lets the Tornado scream into battle as low as 50 feet above the ground

Swing wings give the jet maximum speed for a safe escape after its bombing run

Targets are spotted by the **Laser Range Finder**

Fuel tanks

Alarm anti-radar missiles wrecks enemy air defence by locking onto enemy radar beams and destroying the source

The main weapon of the Tornado's campaign - the Airfield wrecking **JP233 bomb** which craters runways and scatters mines to hinder repairs

TRB 199 twin engines take the jet to more than twice the speed of sound at high altitudes

Underwing Electronic Count Measure pods - which relea flares and chaff to confuse enemy radar and missiles

JP233 RUNWAY DENIAL SYSTEM

1 Tornado GR1 drops over 400 delayed action mines plus 60 cratering bombs from an altitude of 200 ft.

2 Cratering bombs land by parachute and penetrate tarmac before exploding

3 Delayed action mines hinder runway repair team

The terrifying Tornados: A British Top Gun pilot, sporting a "Free Kuwait" badge stands in front of his jet on the Saudi runway. From low-level bombing runs on enemy airfields to air cover for Allied troops in the sand, the Tornados have proved their high-tech battle ability. As the graphics show, they are a deadly sky weapon

Sea Patrol: A Royal Navy Lynx, one of the most deadly military machines of the war, flies past HMS London in the shimmering blue waters of the Gulf.

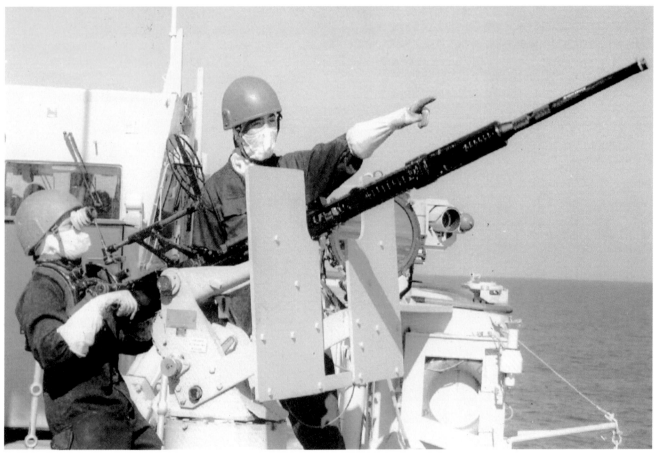

War at Sea: Two U.S. carriers and their escorts patrol Gulf waters.
Below left: Weapons operators on HMS Cardiff check the skyline.
Above left: A fighter takes off from the USS John F. Kennedy.

Ready for Saddam's frontline. British engineers of the 7th Armoured Brigade blow up a mine shield during training in the dunes

Desert Storm and desert calm. Above: Desert Rats launch an assault from a Puma helicopter. Right: A marine writes home from Heartbreak Hotel and, far right, men of the 1st Staffs Regt test their firepower.

Keeping Cool: Woman
trooper from
101 Airborne tries to
keep dry in the Saudi
heat. Right: Desert Rats
train in their chemical
attack suits in the desert.

Staying Cool: Desert
Rat showers in the
blistering Saudi heat.
Left: Father Christmas
arrives in the desert...
without his reindeer.

Ready for the challenge of war. A Challenger tank storms through the sands...and Sapper Alan Flaherty, 24, of the 39th Royal Engineers proudly carries the flag.

"The centre is manned 24 hours a day with up to 50 officers working 12-hour shifts. Grey computer terminals give access to the minute details of each aircraft and its contents, the names of the crew, its location, destination and estimated time of arrival, all flashed up in seconds.

"Scarlet telephones with banks of switches give secure communications to other command posts. White files stamped Top Secret contain the latest classified data on the airlift. Artificial lighting is subdued to cast a shadowy blue hue over the computers. The only concession to the 20th Century in this futuristic setting are the half-empty mugs of cold coffee on every desk.

Bottjer says, "We have moved the equivalent of an entire city the size of Norman, Oklahoma, 7,000 miles, including not only the people but also their cars and trucks, food, retail stock and household furnishing.

"A British equivalent would be moving Maidstone or Barrow-in-Furness to Saudi Arabia in five weeks."

So many American women were being sent to the Gulf they were being nicknamed Mom's Army. The estimated 11,000 servicewomen fulfilled a variety of roles. They flew huge cargo planes and Huey helicopters, maintained tanks, handled petrol and water supplies, drove trucks and worked in intelligence. Women made up 11 per cent of America's 2.1 million military personnel.

By law they were not allowed to serve in combat positions but the women were ready for a fight. One, Lieutenant Stephanie Shaw, 25, who controlled flight missions for jet fighters, told Philip Finn of the Daily Express: "I can fly that F-15 just as well as any man."

Captain Leola Davis, in charge of a heavy maintenance company which fixed everything from tanks to jeeps, said: "I volunteered for the army, not the Girl Scouts."

Many were mothers too, and leaving home for the Gulf tugged at the heart strings. Medical Officer Lieutenant Caroline Roaf said the toughest moment in her life was kissing her six-year-old daughter goodbye, not knowing if she would see her again.

It was predicted that the Americans would have at least 150,000 men and women on the ground in the Gulf by October. There were fears that the desert heat would melt radio wires and the circuits for electronic missile guidance systems.

Few experts believed predictions that if war broke out it would last only three days. They foresaw a drawn-out engagement which could prove one of the nastiest that Western fighting

men had ever been asked to face.

Estimated casualties ranged from 30,000 to 100,000, but no one really knew.

On Tuesday September 11, Mrs Thatcher called a War Cabinet meeting in Downing Street. Among those present were Defence Secretary Tom King, Foreign Office Minister William Waldegrave, Attorney General Sir Patrick Mayhew and the Chief of the Defence Staff, Marshal of the RAF Sir David Craig.

Hours after the meeting the Prime Minister issued a "prepare for war" instruction to the military High Command. She ordered defence chiefs to send a huge fighting machine to Saudi Arabia consisting of 7,000 ground troops and at least 100 tanks. It would be the biggest movement of British forces since the Falklands. Military planners were given three days to present the details.

The package would vastly increase Britain's commitment of £1 million a day spent on the 39 Jaguar, Tornado and Nimrod aircraft, 3,000 men already on station and 12 warships and support vessels.

Saddam sneered at the build-up. He taunted President George Bush over America's failure in the Vietnam War. "The air forces will not carry out a battle in this land, despite their technology," he said. "The last power that fought this were the people of Vietnam. The Americans will be disastrously defeated. Their dens in the region

Women at war: Americans Lt Cecilia Knecht (right) and Lt Matthas of the US Attack Helicopter battalion in Saudi Arabia

'The children of Iraq are dying because they are being deprived of their food and milk and medicine. The trade embargo is depriving my nation.'

Saddam Hussein

will be wiped out if they dare a military challenge."

But he said for the first time that the UN trade ban was beginning to bite. "Children in Iraq are dying because of a foolish decision taken by certain people. Babies are being deprived of their food and milk and medicine." "The trade embargo on Iraq is depriving my nation."

In Britain it was claimed that Iraq, which had lost 1 billion in oil revenues since the clampdown, had a stockpile of grain and meat.

Saddam, in a series of increasingly hysterical Koran-quoting TV statements, repeatedly warned the allies that they faced humiliating defeat in the desert if they attempt to confront Iraq by force.

He made it plain again and again that he had no intention of retreating from Kuwait. It was futile, he insisted, to attempt to restore the situation which existed before the invasion. He appealed to the entire Arab world to join him in opposing the "invaders who had desecrated the land of Mecca".

"The believers will overcome the non-believers," he raged. "Victory will come soon. God will certainly defeat the invaders, and the heads of the traitors" he meant the Arab nations who had ranged against him "will fall from their shoulders."

Even allowing for the often ill-translated hyperbole of the Arabic language, it was a lurid threat. And his words found a hearing among the more zealous ranks of Islam. There were fears that Iran, despite its professed anti-Iraqi stance, might send forces to Baghdad or allow oil to pass through its territory.

Religious leader Ayatollah Khameini said on Teheran Radio: "The struggle against American aggression, its greed, its plans and policies in the Persian Gulf, will be counted as Holy War in the cause of Allah and anyone who is killed on that path is a martyr. We are vehemently opposed to America's presence in the Persian Gulf as well as its increasing greed and its shameless policy in the region."

Khameini was head of Iran's old guard and opposed President Rafsanjani's attempts to improve relations with the West. Whitehall feared that his words could hold up any release of hostages in Beirut. British diplomats had been holding discussions with Teheran aimed at freeing Terry Waite, John McCarthy and Jack Mann.

China and the Yemen said they would send food to Baghdad. But Britain and America took heart when the Syrian president ordered another 10,000 of his soldiers and 300 tanks into Saudi Arabia.

The report came as the Iraqi newsagency warned of attacks against the US and its supporters, including Britain. They said such moves were a natural reaction to the "crimes and insults" against Islam. This could mean industrial sabotage, missile attacks on airlines or even the biological contamination of water supplies.

On Friday September 14, Mrs Thatcher played another trump card. The Desert Rats and their Challenger tanks were going to the Gulf.

lways at the back of military minds were the hostages. The weapons being stockpiled in the desert might be turned against the innocent captives forming Iraq's human shield.

At least Saddam was allowing the women and children out, and they began arriving in the first weeks of September with some rare tales to tell.

Among them was the Stuart Lockwood, the plucky boy star of Saddam's hostage film, who had boarded Iraqi Airways Flight 237 bound for London via Paris on the evening of September 2.

The freedom flight hostages had been stranded at Baghdad Airport for nearly seven hours wondering if they would ever take off. The plane had been delayed to await the arrival of American politician Jesse Jackson, said to be bringing home a party of sick hostages after meeting Saddam.

When the jet finally touched down at Heathrow eight hours later the image-concious Jackson swept Stuart up in his arms and carried him down the steps to the tarmac.

The little boy had one thing to say: "I want my daddy back."

With him was his brother Craig, 14, and mother Glenda. She told of the heartbreaking moment when she said farewell to husband Derek at a military installation near Baghdad.

"We are relieved to be home but terribly sad Derek could not come with us," she said. "My heart is still there. It's the same for all the women who have left their husbands behind."

There was sadness too among the waiting relatives at Heathrow who learned that their loved ones were not on the green and white jumbo. Missing was Denise Dyer, an air stewardess stranded in Kuwait aboard the British Airways jet Coniston Water. Iraqi officials had given her two minutes to decide whether or not to board the freedom plane and she gave up her seat to stay with fellow aircrew husband Neil and celebrate their first wedding anniversary.

One young mother had taken the heart-breaking decision to send her children home without her. While they flew to freedom Roselyn Buchan, 28, remained by her husband David's side in the hope that if she was with him he would

not be taken to a military installation.

Sons Christopher, three, and Matthew, 11, were taken to Aberdeen to be cared for by relatives. Their father, 30-year-old administration officer David, had been in Kuwait three years and the family had been planning to return to Britain when the Iraqis invaded.

Foreign Office Minister William Waldegrave boarded the jet and emerged carrying six-year-old Kayleigh Licence, clutching her favourite doll. Another little girl, eight-year-old Rachel Hughes, echoed Stuart Lockwood's words: "I just want my daddy back."

Among the Britons was only one man, soldier Jerry Blears, 31. With him came wife Jackie, son Colin, 10 and daughter Rachel, whose plea to spend her sixth birthday back home with all her family was granted as a "treat" by Saddam.

Some of the freed hostages told how they had feared for their lives. Student Susan Breeze, 19, from Meifod near Welshpool in Powys, had been captured during a desert escape attempt and then moved from one strategic target to another.

"One day it would be a power station, a few days later a factory, next an army camp," she said.

Valerie Faheem arrived back knowing her 57-year-old husband had run out of vital drugs for his heart condition. Electronics company executive Mohammed Faheem and his wife had been passengers on the Coniston Water.

Other flights followed, all carrying their cargoes of relieved but still worried families. Hundreds of British women were grabbing their children and making desperate dashes across the desert from Kuwait to Baghdad to join Iraqi jets waiting to airlift them to Amman on the first stage of their journey home.

One ramshackle fleet of seven buses and two cars completed the 500-mile escape from Kuwait in 14 hours, half the usual time. The 150 women and 156 children who had responded to a BBC World Service call had driven through the wilderness via Basra in 120F temperatures. The buses were stifling with only scraps of summer clothing tied across the windows to protect the children from the sun.

The mothers, fearful of being attacked, had armed themselves with makeshift weapons of spanners, scissors and knitting needles. Bodies of dead refugees littered their route and what little food and water they took with them was soon used up.

Airline and records tycoon Richard Branson pitched in to help fly the families home. When he stepped on to the Gatwick tarmac on September 5 he brought with him Yasmin Ibrahim, cradled in the arms of her mother Ann. Branson broke down in tears as he told how the British-born teacher had been forced to leave hospital in Kuwait two hours after giving birth and then flee the country without her Iraqi husband.

"Every single available plane must be used to take out emergency supplies and bring people back," said Branson an hour after Virgin flight VS 502 touched down in Britain.

There were more tears when the brother and sister team who had set up the Gulf Support Group watched TV footage of a freedom convoy arriving in Baghdad. To their amazement Jonathan and Joanna Copley saw their sister Jane, 27, safe and well.

Despite having access to a vast databank on Gulf hostages they had heard little of Jane since she was stranded in Kuwait on the Coniston Water.

"It's absolutely incredible," said Jonathan, 18. "We've had a few conflicting reports but nothing direct for four weeks now, and now to see her fit

Desert Frontline: Men of America's 82nd Airborne arrive in Saudi Arabia to spearhead the Allied operation

and well...I just hope there are lots of people sharing this moment with me around the country."

Teacher Jane, of Wellington in Somerset had been on her way to Kuala Lumpur to start a new job. Sheffield University student Jonathan said: "She was only supposed to be in Kuwait for an hour and a half."

Office manager Joanna, 29, had given up work to help the group handle more than 1,000 calls a week from its base at the Connaught Rooms in Holborn, London.

As mothers and wives reached safety they told of the 1,000 British men still in hiding in Kuwait.

Bernice Tallboys, 27, from Cheltenham, said: "It's a terrifying situation in the city. The men are dressing up in Arab head-dresses and other native clothes and moving around the streets helped by friendly locals. We used to hide under beds, in lofts, anywhere, if we were warned that Iraqi troops were in the neighbourhood."

Teacher Joanna Restall, 29, from Brighton, said she pretended to be Irish to travel from Kuwait to Baghdad then on to Amman. "I was frightened to say I was British, especially after some of Margaret Thatcher's comments," she said. "Some of the British people there would be very grateful if she would just lock herself in a cupboard and keep quiet for a few weeks, or months.

"Life in Kuwait was terrifying. I feared I would end up in a military camp. I never thought I'd live through it. People are scared in the city, particularly the men. They hardly go out. The shops are closed and there are wrecked cars everywhere. It's like a ghost town."

Miriam Tyler, 29, another evacuee, said: "We have been living in fear, hiding in cupboards, behind water tanks, under staircases and in roof spaces.

"There were 15 of us, British women and children, hiding in one house. We dared not go outside. We could hear Iraqi soldiers banging on doors and smashing windows and shouting for

British people to give themselves up. We genuinely believed that we could be taken out and killed.

"It was hard on the little ones. I spent periods of half a day at a time hiding in a wardrobe with my children, all the time in fear that we would be found. I held my hand over my baby's mouth in case he cried. "How they never found us I do not know. But I thank God that they didn't."

Even the children had their tales to tell. Six-year-old Adam Hozaifa said: "The bombs made me very frightened. A shell hit the wall of our house while we were inside. We tried to get out but could not. The dust got into my eyes but they're all right now."

Ten-year-old Tariq Alahou said: "All the shop windows were smashed in Kuwait and cars were burnt out. I was really scared soldiers would take me hostage. My dad's last words to me were, Be brave son and look after your mother and sisters. I will see you soon."

Suzanne Turvey, 18, told how Iraqi soldiers had forced her to lead them to her father. Suzanne and two other women were picked up in Kuwait for breaking a curfew as they made their way to join a convoy hoping to return to Britain.

Troops and two men claiming to be diplomats quizzed her for seven hours, warning: "Tell us where your father is or you will not be going anywhere."

Said Suzanne: "They kept asking me over and over again where my father was. The message was very clear. Unless I was prepared to shop my father, I would be staying. I held out as long as possible. But I thought if I kept refusing to say anything things would get worse for me and dad."

Finally, tired and scared, she gave the address in Kuwait where her father John, an oil refinery worker, had hidden since the invasion.

Suzanne was taken in a coach with her father and other hostages under armed guard to Baghdad. She was permitted to hug him in a tearful farewell before he was taken away to a hotel.

THE GULF SUPPORT GROUP: A HELPING HAND FOR FAMILIES OF HOSTAGES

The Gulf Support Group was founded to help relatives of the hostages held in Iraq and the Britons in hiding in Kuwait. It grew out of two separate groups formed at the beginning of the crisis, one by Bristol Tory MP Robert Hayward and the other by brother and sister team Jonathan and Joanna Copley.

The Copleys' 27-year-old sister Jane had been on her way to start a new teaching job in Kuala Lumpur when she was trapped with the other passengers and crew of the BA jumbo jet Coniston Water stranded at Kuwait Airport.

Jane eventually left Kuwait as part of a desert freedom convoy along with 500 other women and children, but Joanna car-

ried on her work from London's Connaught Rooms even after her sister had returned home.

She gave up her £15,000 job as office manager for a computer company to work a seven day week at the head of 150 volunteers handling up to 1,000 calls a week.

One of the most rewarding parts of her work, she said, was forcing banks, building societies and the DSS to realise the financial difficulties of the hostages and their families.

"I have to admit one of the more satisfying parts of this job has been kicking smug men in dark suits and making them wince," she said.

Suzanne's mother Sandra Turvey said at her home in Barrow-in-Furness: ""My daughter did the right thing. She was brave to hold out for so long. I am proud of her and I have told her she shouldn't feel badly at what she had to do."

The Bride of Baghdad, Debbie Hayes, whose white wedding in Iraq was seen by millions on TV, also flew back without her new husband. Debbie denied she had been pressured into marrying as a propaganda stunt. "We decided to marry at the start of the invasion, that's all," she said after being reunited with her parents in Humberside.

Tony Wilbraham, a 50-year-old civil engineer, was actually hauled off a jet bound for Britain because Iraqi troops refused to believe he had lung cancer. His wife, Maureen, 50, sacrificed her place on the plane to stay with him.

Relatives in their home town of Blackpool were desperately hoping Tony would be allowed home. His mother Madge said: "This is the cruellest blow of all. To let us believe our son was on his way home to us and then dash our hopes is deplorable. There just doesn't seem to be any end to our ordeal. I just want to know that Tony is all right and have him back so he can get proper treatment."

For every tale of suffering there was one of hope and even humour. French TV reporter Patrick Poivre d'Arvor smuggled 18-month-old Florian Barbut out of Iraq in a TRAVEL BAG.

Patrick was covering the plight of Western hostages in Baghdad when he told Florian's father of the idea. Andre Barbut agreed and gave Saddam's youngest hostage half a baby's bottle of champagne to stop him crying, then packed him in the reporter's hand luggage.

But little Florian woke up and started screaming when he arrived at Baghdad Airport. The TV crew surrounded Patrick and began talking loudly to cover up the cries.

Florian fell asleep again and the team flew to Amman, where Patrick telephoned the baby's mother Karoline and told her: "Meet me in Paris I have a present for you."

Karoline said: "When we met, Patrick handed Florian to me. It was amazing. Words failed me. I wanted to give this brave reporter a present, so I made him Florian's godfather."

The champagne might had been flowing for Florian, but it had dried up for British Ambassador Michael Weston and his envoys trapped in their embassy in Kuwait with a cage of canaries and three stray cats who had wandered in off the street.

All the fresh vegetables and fruit had been eaten. The diplomats were living on canned food, eggs and bottled water. Pinafore-clad Mr Weston

'If anything happens to the hostages we could do what we did at Nuremberg and prosecute the requisite people for their totally uncivilised and brutal behaviour.'

Margaret Thatcher

was doing the cooking.

Foreign Secretary Douglas Hurd, in Abu Dhabi, used a diplomatic radio link to get through to the embassy. "The Ambassador is light-hearted about many aspects, but no one should get the idea that this is a picnic," he said "These are people in a dangerous and difficult situation. They volunteered to get into that and it is immensely important they stay in touch with the British community and show solidarity in remaining."

Mr Weston told reporters over the telephone: "It's very hot and very sticky without the air-conditioning. We have all had some sleepless nights. But our morale remains good and our spirits are sky high."

The embassy's electricity came from an oil-fired generator. There was a small fridge but it was only kept on for a few hours at a time to save fuel. Armed Iraqi troops, who guarded the embassy 24 hours a day, never tried to interfere. But from bedrooms at the top of the two-storey compound the diplomats could see mortars and machine guns trained constantly on them.

The scene outside the embassy was described by an American woman in hiding in Kuwait who claimed that guerrilla action had been stepped up. "There is strong resistance," she reported. "Young and old men and women are fighting to get their country back."

**Desert despair:
Queen Noor and
Richard Branson visit a
refugee camp**

As Baghdad threatened to jail anyone caught trying to escape to Saudi Arabia, Foreign Office Minister Waldegrave praised the bravery of British desert "Pimpernels", often disguised in Arab dress, who were helping other trapped Britons. They were also acting as the eyes and ears of Michael Weston and his besieged embassy staff.

Mrs Thatcher warned Saddam against harming any of the male hostages forced to stay behind. She pledged that Iraqi leaders would face a Nuremberg-style war crimes court if a single hostage died even as a result of a Western military strike.

In an hour-long TV-am interview with David Frost she insisted that Saddam's attempt to surround himself with a human shield of hostages would not stop the West launching a strike.

It would be "a decision of anguish", she admitted. "If anything happened to those hostages we could do what we did at Nuremberg and prosecute the requisite people for their totally uncivilised and brutal behavour." The Prime Minister said a blacklist was being compiled of Saddam's leading officers who commited any criminal acts.

Asked about the possible fate of the hostages if war broke out, she said: "We are prepared to take any action that is necessary. If you allow the

taking of hostages, terrible as it is, to determine your own action against a dictator he has won. All anyone else with similar ambitions would ever do is to take hostages knowing that other people would never take action."

Mrs Thatcher's TV appearance brought an immediate response from the Iraqis. They branded her a "barking grey-haired old woman" who had "lost her psychological balance".

But her handling of the crisis sent her popularity soaring. William Hill moved the Tories from 11-10 outsiders to 8-11 favourites to win an election, with Labour drifting from 5-6 to evens.

And a Sunday Express survey showed that 65 per cent thought Mrs Thatcher the most capable leader of Britain in the crisis compared to 20 per cent for Mr Kinnock.

A thousand British women and children fled before Saddam announced the end of charter flights taking them to Amman. The move meant that any more refugees would have to make the arduous overland journey to Jordan. That set the scene for a new magnitude of suffering.

Like most of the rich Gulf states Kuwait depended on imported Third World labour. Thousands of Indians, Asian and South-East Asians were employed as servants, labourers and general menials. They too wanted to leave the occupied state but they did not have the backing of money, diplomacy and an active media to see fair play done. They were on their own, and they streamed to the border of Jordan to find a nightmare waiting.

The refugees were placed in vast transit camps. The worst of these was a hell-hole called Shalaan. The stench of this tent city fouled the desert wind. There was human waste, disease, despair and the smell of death.

The shanty town lay in the heat-blasted no-man's-land between Iraq and Jordan. Each day scores of people collapsed from dehydration and disease. Screaming children, their skin blistered by the sun, stood in their own waste. Every time a truck arrived with food or water there was a riot. People tore at each other to get their hands on a loaf of bread.

Attempts to provide sanitation had failed and the camp had become an open sewer. At first in one area refugees had queued 400 yards for a solitary portable toilet. But diarrhoea was rife and no one could wait. Half-naked men and women wandered around, too defeated to retain their dignity. Exhausted medical staff struggled to cope.

Thousands more refugees arrived daily in

convoys of buses and cars. They tied blankets or clothing together and hung them on pieces of wood to form the only shelter from the 120F heat. Some split cardboard boxes and fixed them together to make ramshackle homes. Mothers with young children sat staring blankly ahead, waiting for their daily ration of food.

Richard Branson and British newsmen including the Daily Express's Paul Thompson experienced the despair of such camps at first hand. Branson, visibly moved, pledged relief supplies after a plea by Queen Noor of Jordan, who said adults and children were dying in the camps, dysentery was rife and cholera was breaking out.

She warned of even greater human tragedy unless there was massive and urgent international help. The American-born wife of King Hussein made her plea to the British public during an interview with Jimmy Young on Radio 2.

America had already promised to send rice, vegetable oil and wheat flour to the refugees.

Already 60,000 refugees were in two border camps and the numbers were increasing daily. Queen Noor feared that they could reach two million. International Red Cross organiser Bernard Kaspar warned of "an absolute catastrophe" if a huge international airlift was not organised.

There were 500 casualties a day from a lack of adequate water supply, dysentery, viral diseases and scorpion bites, he said. Fresh emergency accommodation was being arranged at Azraq, 60 miles from Amman, but Kaspar said up to 200,000 could still flee from Iraq.

"We are already hopelessly overcrowded," he said. "If it gets worse we face a catastrophe. These people are not refugees but ordinary working folk like the rest of us, forced to leave everying."

The International Organisation for Migration announced that it had set up a 25 million airlift, with 72 flights from Amman over the following two weeks. Branson ferried in 25,000 blankets for the unfortunates waiting in the camps and picked up the £100,000 bill.

The cost of the crisis began to worry the West. William Waldegrave was off to Rome to urge European Community foreign secretaries to put up £5 billion in relief aid for Jordan and Turkey, the latter hard-hit by the crisis since it shut down its oil pipeline.

The bills were piling up for Britain, too. The cost of the UK's deployments and constant Gulf patrols was put as high as £400 million for the first month alone by defence experts.

"Our contribution is costing our taxpayers a great deal more than other countries, who should contribute a good deal more in other ways," said a Whitehall source.

The Saudi government agreed to meet the fuel costs of the British forces and Defence Secretary Tom King said: "We will be discussing cost-sharing further with our friends in the Gulf." He was later to stress: "We need to see the successful liberation of Kuwait... but the clear assurance it will stay liberated."

Japan, which under its post-war constitution could not make a military contribution, had already promised up to £1 billion towards the cost of Desert Shield.

'We need to see not only the successful liberation of Kuwait, but the clear assurance it will stay liberated.'

Tom King

War fears: Thousands of refugees flee the war zone in the hope of finding safety in Jordan

Mrs Thatcher criticised Britain's NATO and European partners for dragging their feet over the crisis. With West Germany clearly her main target, she virtually accused them of talking tough but doing nothing. President Bush warned that America's richest allies would be asked to help pay for his desert strike force.

The President and Mikhail Gorbachev met in Helsinki and came up with a joint statement after seven hours of talks. It was a show of co-operation unthinkable during the bad old days of the Cold War. Their mutual message to Saddam was: Get out of Kuwait, or else.

They also told him to restore the ousted government and free all hostages. The American and Russian leaders said they both wanted a peaceful settlement brought about by the rigorous enforcement of UN sanctions.

"We will be united against Iraq's aggression as long as this crisis exists," they declared. "We are determined to see this aggression end and if the current steps fail to end it we are prepared to consider additional ones consistent with the UN Charter. We must demonstrate beyond any doubt that aggression cannot and will not pay."

The two leaders refused to discuss the nature of future measures, but the UN Charter allowed the use of force in defence of a member state.

President Gorbachev was careful to spell out that openly-promised Soviet support would be limited to "strict compliance" with Security Council resolutions. But he warned his former ally: "If Saddam provokes military action then the result would be a tragedy first and foremost for the Iraqi people themselves, for the whole of the region and the whole of the world." Saddam was driving Iraq into "a dead end", he said.

The joint communique also pledged an initiative to bring peace to the Middle East after the Gulf crisis was over. Mr Bush refused to bow to Iraqi pressure and link a solution to the Kuwait crisis with an Arab-Israeli settlement.

The American President had succeeded in calming Kremlin fears that the Gulf crisis could lead to a permanent American presence in Saudi Arabia within easy striking distance of the Soviet Union's restive southern frontier. But he failed on two vital counts.

Mr Gorbachev stressed that he had no plans to send Soviet military forces to support Desert Shield, and he repeatedly stressed the need for a political solution.

"We may have a difference over that," President Bush admitted. President Gorbachev also failed to promise the immediate withdrawal of 150 Soviet military advisers in Baghdad.

The two leaders preferred to stress the new spirit of East-West cooperation and their unity in the face of Iraq's invasion. "The statement should tell Saddam that the Soviet Union and the United States are in essential agreement," said President Bush. "It will say to him that he is not going to divide us or divide other countries."

In Britain Parliament was recalled from its long summer recess for the first time since the Falklands crisis of 1982. Foreign Secretary Douglas Hurd warned company bosses that anyone caught breaching sanctions against Iraq faced severe penalties fines, or even jail. He told a packed chamber that it was up to the UN Security Council to decide if there was a humanitarian need for food supplies and added: "We cannot allow Saddam Hussein to manipulate this subject to his own advantage."

Mr Hurd made it clear that sanctions were vital in preventing a military conflict. Oil exports from Iraq had been virtually stopped. "Saddam won't run out of oil, but he should run out of money," he said. "We have to build up pressures until they become intolerable."

He stressed that although the immediate danger of conflict had passed there was still "anxiety and tension in the air". The Foreign Secretary warned those who were calling for compromise that Saddam could not be allowed to go "smiling home out of Kuwait with two islands and an oilfield in his pocket."

Labour's foreign spokesman Gerald Kaufman said his party had so far backed the Government's actions. He cautioned: "We shall not be voting for a blank cheque for whatever action may be taken in the future." Still, Labour approved of the sanctions policy and would support an air blockade of Iraq if the Security Council agreed.

Kuwait's Crown Prince, Sheikh Saadal-Sabah, said in London that his country's ruling family would not go into exile as part of any peace plan.

'Saddam won't run out of oil . . . but he should run out of money! We must build up pressures until they are intolerable.'

Douglas Hurd

CHAPTER

4

THE GULF

WAR

'Nearly 50 years ago the Desert Rats were preparing to fight in the sand. It seems proper that we should be chosen to go back to the desert to defuse this crisis'

Brigadier Patrick Cordingley

In a huge cobbled yard at Fallingbostel, West Germany, the Desert Rats of Britain's 7th Armoured Brigade prepared to swap the rolling plains of Europe for the searing sands of Arabia. Within two weeks they would kiss their loved ones goodbye and, with their 120 Challenger tanks, join the biggest mobilisation of British land forces since World War II.

President Bush was overjoyed when Mrs

Thatcher rang him from Downing Street and announced that the descendants of Montgomery's Desert Rats, who routed Rommel in North Africa, were on their way. He called the news the "icing on the cake" and pledged to urge other allies to play their part and join America's Gulf force, now standing at 160,000 with more flooding in.

As the two leaders agreed to meet in New York for a UN conference, Canada promised to send a

Man in the bunker: Air-Chief Marshall, Sir Patrick Hine, who directed operations in a twilight world of high-tech communications, under the Buckinghamshire countryside.

squadron of CF-18 fighters and 450 military personnel to join its two warships and a supply vessel already heading for the danger zone. Italy announced it was sending a fourth warship and eight Tornados.

The US Navy fired shots across an Iraqi oil tanker's bows and boarded it with the help of Australian sailors. The tanker, which had refused US commands to stop in the Gulf of Oman for a sanctions-busting check, was found to be empty and allowed to proceed to Basra.

Royal Navy and merchant ships were preparing to carry out the eight-week job of moving military hardware from Germany to the Gulf. The reinforcements would double the cost of Britain's Gulf contribution from £1 million to £2 million a day, with the start-up bill soaring from £75 million to £100 million. It would have a "very severe impact" on the military budget, said Defence Secretary Tom King, after a War Cabinet meeting headed by Mrs Thatcher. The British Government expected Saudi Arabia to share the cost.

The movement of troops and supplies was a challenge for the top brass. Their mission was to ship the equivalent of a city the size of Canterbury to Saddam's front door. Already the Navy's floating supermarket, the Royal Fleet Auxiliary Fort Grange, was at sea supplying British and allied ships with food and ammunition drawn from 42,000 lines, more than four times the range offered by Marks & Spencer. Her cargo included 750,000 sheets of greaseproof paper, 50 tons of potatoes, 3 tons of apples, 3 tons of cabbage, 72,000 eggs, 13,000 frozen chickens, 11,000 tins of baked beans and 39,000 toilet rolls. She was nicknamed RFA Grangeways.

Another vessel bound for the war zone was the Falklands veteran Sir Tristram, which was to lead a flotilla of four craft taking Challenger tanks.

Back at Fallingbostel, Brigadier Patrick

Cordingley, the 7th's commanding officer, was finalising arrangements for putting his men into the front line. Flanked by his officers and sporting a red Desert Rat's badge, a gift from a veteran of Monty's victory over the Afrika Korps, he said: "It is almost 50 years ago that the Desert Rats were preparing to fight in the sand. It seems proper that we should be chosen to go back to the desert to defuse this crisis.

"Every single one of us is exceptionally proud to have been chosen. We would have been surprised if we had been left out, because we are well-trained and suited to coping with the task. We have pride, equipment and morale, the things the British Army is famous for.

"Our Challenger tanks are good and in desert conditions will be excellent. Challenger is the best-protected tank in the world. We have been training for chemical warfare and the men have exercised in protective suits in 30 degrees on the plains in Canada. But I hope the Gulf crisis does not come to war. We are going there to deter aggression."

Nearly three quarters of the brigade had already served in Northern Ireland. One of them, Private Stephen Williams, said: "At least where we are going, with someone like Saddam, we know who the enemies are. In Northern Ireland we had no idea. It could have been anyone on the street."

The Rats fiercely defended their Challengers. The 60-ton war machine was being portrayed in a stream of reports as a death trap in the desert.

It was originally designed for the Shah of Iran just before he was toppled in the late 1970s. Now critics were claiming that the Vickers-built tank was slower than modern rivals and could not shoot straight. A BBC documentary alleged that the Challenger was a danger to its crew.

"I can lick the pants off anything anyone puts in front of me," retorted one sergeant. "I have just

THE CHALLENGER: A TANK AT HOME IN THE UNFORGIVING DESERT

By a strange quirk of fate Britain's tanks in the Gulf were the only ones in the area designed specifically for desert warfare.

The Challenger, developed from the Chieftain, was originally built as the Shir in the mid-1970s for service in the Shah of Iran's army. The Shah was deposed and Challenger was deployed on the North German plain for 15 years. But it adapted superbly to the desert conditions.

It has a crew of four, is powered by a massive Perkins diesel engine and has a top speed of around 56kph. One revolutionary feature of the tank is a dual horsepower selection system which allows the driver to opt for an 800hp cruise rating or a 1200hp battle rating, a feature which gives improved reliability and greater operational range.

The tank is armed with a standard 120mm rifled gun which

has a range of 2 miles. It also has two 7.62 machine guns and is fully protected against germ and chemical attack.

The Challenger carries almost twice as much fuel as the Iraqis' T72s and is 30 per cent heavier with a combat weight of 62,000kg 60 tons. Much of this comes from the Chobham armour which makes it the best-protected tank in the world. The armour has been upgraded in the Gulf against the threat of long-range artillery.

One worry for the Challenger crews, who firmly believed that their tank was the best in the world, had always been its gunnery. The night-fighting capabilities of the Allies' tanks were extremely advanced but Challenger consistently failed in NATO gunnery contests and was eventually withdrawn after a string of defeats by America's M1A Abrams and the German Leopard.

A British Challenger tank rumbles off a cargo ship in the Gulf.

come back from gunnery school and we were hitting every target."

The military editor of the authoritative Jane's Defence Weekly, Chris Foss, added: "There has been a lot of distortion and misunderstanding about the Challenger. If I was going to war tomorrow I would not mind going out in a Challenger. I would prefer it to almost any other NATO tank."

Other experts pointed out that the Challenger had heavy armour, a powerful 120mm gun, the best night vision and was much more fuel efficient than rivals.

By now the tanks had been repainted in their desert camouflage. The Army called the new livery "grey stone". The men said it was pink. That gave rise to suggestions that the Rats should henceforth be known as the Pink Panzers. One driver, 22-year-old Stevie Kelly, said: "I don't mind what colour it is. No one will call us the Pink Panzies!"

The Army top brass was putting out a new order: "No sex please you're British officers." The message was for a husband and wife team of Army doctors who were preparing for the Gulf.

Captain Vanessa England, 25, was determined to go to the Middle East but it meant she would be one of only three women among the 7,000 men of 7th Armoured Brigade. The Army drew the line at Vanessa and husband Captain Mike England, 26, living as man and wife. Their CO at 1st Armoured Field Ambulance, Lt Col Malcolm Braithwaite, said: "If Mike and Vanessa want to be in a tent together they will have to share with a dozen others." And if Vanessa wanted to shower or change, she would be told to muck in with the chaps.

Mike and Vanessa weren't the only ones having difficulties. The entire mail system between the US and the war zone had been clogged up with love letters from wives and girlfriends to the men in the front line. In one week alone 38 tons of mail arrived at Heathrow in three freighters.

The British end of the Gulf build-up, code-named Operation Granby, was orchestrated from a massive modern bunker below the Buckinghamshire countryside, 4,000 miles from Saddam's front line. Here Britain's joint commander Air Chief Marshall Sir Paddy Hine, held court in a twilight world of hi-tech communication.

A stone's throw from the base where Bomber Harris masterminded the bombing of Nazi Germany, Sir Paddy, overall boss of all Britain's Gulf forces, was to take vital decisions in the heart of the 80 million nuclear bunker. Now designated Joint HQ, the War Room would give Sir Paddy instant access to commanders in the field and a telephone hotline gave him the ear of Mrs Thatcher or Defence Secretary Tom King in seconds. Accompanied by his Director of Operations, Air Vice Marshal Dick Johns, and assistant directors from the Army, RAF and RN, Sir Paddy surveyed a room manned by senior officers who sat at a battery of screens linked to military computers being set up across the Gulf. At the touch of a button they would be able to send messages to local commanders or share vital information.

The bunker, opened in April 1989 after seven years of complex construction work designed to leave it impenetrable, was proof against electronic jamming and biological, chemical or nuclear attack. Contractors dug out 161,000 cubic metres of soil to create the hole and the bunker needed 250,000 tons of cement and 2,000 miles of steel reinforcement rods weighing 10,000 tonnes.

Yet all that showed was a grass-covered mound five miles from the Home Counties commuter

War Room: The control centre at High Wycombe, where staff work around the clock, sending hi-tech messages to commanders in the desert.

town of High Wycombe. Deep below was a four-level warren of operation cells, canteens and dormitories. To enter an officer had to pass through a series of steel airtight doors several inches thick.

The bunker had 450 beds, enough for the 500 personnel working round-the-clock shifts. The next floor down was the Operations Centre and below that two floors providing essential services. The hideaway had its own generators, air filters, water and sewerage systems. Heat was provided by a combination of human bodies and conventional heaters.

The bunker was designed at the height of the Cold War with the Soviets in mind. Clocks which used to tell British commanders the time in Moscow were now set on Gulf time. Maps of the North German plain and Eastern Europe were replaced by maps of the Middle East.

One of the most vital high-tech links was that between the bunker and the Pentagon. For across the Atlantic the awesome military build-up rumbled on relentlessly.

An impressive piece of military hardware, much admired by British officers in the bunker, was the tank-busting Apache helicopter with its laser-guided Hellfire missiles and multiple rocket pods. The Apache was one of the main offensive weapons against Iraqi tanks.

Sunday Express journalist Rowena Webster went to Fort Rucker in Alabama to see the Apache in action. She reported:

"Here in Alabama, Wild West imagery still maintains a powerful hold on the American military. Words like fort, cavalry, ambush and Apache are more commonplace than Ford and Coca-Cola. It is here at Fort Rucker that the modern American cavalrymen learn how to ride their modern mounts into battle.

"The US Army pilots put their Apache anti-tank helicopters through their paces prior to deployment in the Gulf. Many men and machines have already been despatched. More will follow.

"Pilots have named the Apache – the Prince of Darkness. It is built for surprise, stealth, speed and firepower, the essential ingredients of ambush.

"The Apache's manoeuvrability, precision-targeting and powerful weapons-delivery system enables pilots to strike enemy armour with great accuracy and from long range. The Apache's night vision system also allows pilots to continue fighting effectively in the dark.

"Here they just don't like the Apaches, they worship and adore them. These men are not Pentagon politicians trying to justify the spending of billions of dollars in developing and acquiring the aircraft. They are the fighting men at the sharp end, men whose lives depend on the machine. Army aviators extol its virtues in customarily colourful prose: 'It's the largest can of whip-ass in the world.'

"The pilots praise the helicopter's survivability. They must be able to destroy the enemy but live to tell the tale. For that reason the Apache is built to keep flying even after sustaining considerable battle damage. Pilot Tony Kraay, who flew Cobra helicopters in Vietnam, said, The comparison would be like driving a 1934 Ford then and a Ferrari now. We say it's about as much fun as you can have without having a girl up there.'

"Apache pilots learn to fly the helicopter a few feet from the ground, hugging the contours of the land, using trees and hills for cover as they seek out the enemy without being spotted themselves.

"From its fat nose to the tail rotor 58ft away the ugly Apache has been designed for battle, not for looks. My wife says it looks as though it should be pulling a trailer,' said one pilot.

"But once airborne, they say, the ugly duckling turns into a lethal swan."

Other forces were entering the arena. French President Francois Mitterrand ordered 4,000 legionnaires with their tanks and warplanes into the Gulf. It was in retaliation for the sacking by Iraqi troops of the French Embassy residence in Kuwait City. "I always said that further aggression by Iraq was possible and that one would have to respond," said Mitterrand.

Iraqi troops had also briefly detained the US consul in Kuwait along with envoys from Ireland and Australia when soldiers invaded the Canadian ambassador's residence during a meeting. Troops also entered Belgian and Dutch offices. After a protest from Mitterrand the Iraqis released a senior French diplomat grabbed in raids on Western compounds.

The French President's announcement raised France's troop commitment in the Gulf to more than 13,000 soldiers, airmen and sailors. He was sending a regiment of 48 combat helicopters and 1,100 men, an armoured regiment of 48 AMX 10 tanks, an infantry regiment of five companies with anti-tank weapons and a company of engineer troops from the anti-air missile section.

Mitterrand announced that Iraq's four military attaches at its Paris Embassy were being expelled, along with Iraqi intelligence agents who did not have diplomatic status.

But France would not abandon its long-standing refusal to allow its troops to operate under the command of a non-Frenchman. That was one of the fundamental reasons why the country left NATO's integrated military command.

West German Chancellor Helmut Kohl announced that Germany was providing £1.1 billion in immediate support for military operations in the Gulf.

Among the first Western political casualties of the Gulf crisis was America's top airman, 53-year-old General Michael Dugan, sacked by President Bush for threatening to "decapitate" Iraq with air raids.

Dugan declared that warplanes would level Baghdad and "wipe out" Saddam if a Gulf war erupted. "Because Saddam is a one-man show in Iraq he ought to be the focus of our efforts," said the US Air Force Chief of Staff.

Dugan said a squadron of 20 deadly F-117 Stealth fighter-bombers had been flying missions every night for two weeks simulating strikes at Saddam. The thrust would be downtown Baghdad.

"This bombing would not be nibbling at the edges. If I want to hurt you it would be at home,

not out in the woods some place," he said. The outburst angered the White House. A spokesman said Mr and Mrs Bush, devoted parents and grandparents, were "deeply affronted" by the general's declaration that America was prepared to attack civilian targets.

The official reason for the sacking was that General Dugan was not authorised to make such comments. He was the first joint chief of staff to be sacked by America for 40 years. The Defence Department announced that Vice Chief of Staff General John Loh would take Dugan's place pending the announcement of a successor.

In Baghdad, Colonel John Cochrane, Britain's 46-year-old military attache, was given a week to pack his bags. His two support staff, Army Sgt Joe Conway and RAF Sgt Peter Davies were also given their marching orders.

The Iraqis also moved against staff from France, Italy, Spain and Egypt. The moves were in retaliation for a European Community-wide expulsion of Saddam's military henchmen following the illegal Iraqi raids on Western embassies in occupied Kuwait.

"I'm afraid it's what we expected," Mrs Thatcher said in Zurich. "It was totally unjustified, of course, because we had committed no offence at all. We have honoured diplomatic status. This was just retaliation."

Britain had thrown out Iraq's eight-man military team, including a brigadier and a lieutenant colonel, plus 23 Iraqis, mostly students living in Britain. No more Iraqi students were to be allowed in.

In Kuwait, the situation was deteriorating to such an extent that Iraqi troops were slaughtering zoo animals for food, according to the US-based World Society for the protection of animals.

Victor Watkins, the society's regional director in London, said: "There is absolutely no doubt about the truth of these stories. They have come from people who have fled the country, including some of the 40 staff who were employed at the zoo.

"It is an appalling tragedy. This was one of the biggest and the best-run zoos in the Middle East. Immediately before the occupation it held 208 mammals, 493 birds and 34 reptiles including quite a number of animals on the endangered list of species.

"Most of the staff were Asian and seem to have got out of the country. The picture of cruelty they tell of is horrific. Many animals have died or been ill-treated. Soldiers taunted some of the animals in their cages to make them angry before releasing them simply to shoot them. Seventy per

'I always said that further aggression by the Iraqis was possible – and that one would have to respond.'

President Mitterrand

cent of the edible animals like deer and antelope have been eaten by soldiers."

The society claimed that some of the world's finest racehorses and showjumpers, owned by the Emir's family, had either been taken to Baghdad or turned loose to die in the desert.

There were also reports that resistance in Kuwait was now almost non-existent. Refugees Rami Sullman and his wife Galina described street executions and the bombing and burning of all suspected resistance hideouts.

"There has not been a single shot, not a single explosion, for the past three nights. The resistance has been put down totally," said Mr Sullman.

"Every night after the invasion there were shootings and explosions in different parts of the city. The resistance fighters were at work. For a long time the Iraqis were more concerned with establishing their forces. Then they cracked down on the resistance. I personally saw six Kuwaitis hanged in the streets, all suspected freedom fighters."

Rami's wife added: "The mood in Kuwait has changed. Despite the invasion there used to be hope that the city would be freed. But the resistance has ended, now there is only despair. We left a ghost city. Civilians do not walk the streets. Shops, homes and banks are empty and there are few cars because there is no petrol."

Kuwait's ambassador in London, Ghazi al-Rayes, admitted "some difficulties" but said the resistance would be changing tactics.

It emerged that Kuwait was becoming a new homeland for hundreds of thousands of Palestinians, who were moving in to supplant the fleeing Kuwaitis. Fewer than 250,000 native Kuwaitis were left against an estimated 500,000-plus Palestinians. This appeared to be a deliberate Iraqi ploy. Saddam calculated that even the Arab states prepared to go to war against him would be reluctant to move against Palestinians.

More Egyptian troops poured into the Gulf. They had been told by their Interior Minister, Mohammed Abdel-Halim Moussa, that at least 24 of their countrymen had been killed in Iraq trying to flee. Moussa said post mortems showed that some of the victims had been murdered. Iraqi medical documents on the coffins said they had died in "accidents".

The exiled Emir of Kuwait begged the world to set his people free. In an emotional address to foreign ministers at the UN, recalling Haile Selassie's historic appeal to the League of Nations after Mussolini overran Ethiopia, the ousted leader urged the world to stand firm against what he called Iraq's "naked and brutal aggression".

"The fate of my country is in your hands," he said. Sheikh Sabah, with a personal fortune of more than £55 billion, promised to write off interest payments on massive debts owed to Kuwait by Third World countries.

The Emir concluded with a televised message to Kuwaitis in exile or still trying to fight Iraqi troops. "I assure each and every one of you, the Almighty will ultimately restore triumph for us," he said.

There were various peace moves, some more plausible than others.

In London former Tory Prime Minister Edward Heath said on TV that Saddam should be offered a deal to avoid war in the Middle East. He told London Weekend Television's Brian Walden: "Saddam Hussein is not a Hitler. I don't believe he is a Hitler."

Mr Heath insisted that proposals for talks over the disputed Rumaila oilfields, from which Iraq claimed Kuwait was taking more than its share, could not be seen as appeasement.

"What Saddam sees is forces massed against him, so he can't make any further aggression. The UN could always do the same again. This cannot possibly show Saddam that aggression pays."

It was essential, Mr Heath went on, that any deal was struck through Arab mediation with UN and Western forces remaining in place in the region because the Arab countries shared the same desire to avert war.

The Iraqi leader had already got away with a variety of acts without world opinion turning against him, and may have thought he could do the same in Kuwait, said Mr Heath.

"He may have been taken aback by the scale of the operation which has been mounted against him. If so, so much better. It points to the fact that he can make a very rapid turn of policy, still hold the support of his armies and generals and the people, as we have seen from the processions and so on and we could reach agreement about various outstanding things."

Queen Noor of Jordan added her voice to the peace process in an exclusive interview at Amman's royal palace with Daily Express journalist Philippa Kennedy.

"The consequences of war in this area do not bear thinking about," the Queen said. "There have been too many battles fought in distant regions of the world by armies who didn't understand why they were there. It is vital that this does not happen again."

Queen Noor, 39, was anxious not to make any political statement. She was speaking on humanitarian grounds because of what she called the sheer human misery she had witnessed in the

On parade: Twenty thousand U.S. marines gather at Camp Lejune in North Carolina, hours before flying to the Gulf.

refugee camps on Jordan's border with Iraq.

But she feared for the Middle East if the West did not listen to her husband, King Hussein's advice. His 38 years on the throne had given him "a unique and extraordinary feeling for the pulse of the people of the region."

Queen Noor said: "If his good counsel were followed now, the possibilities for peace and stability in this area would certainly be enhanced. He is not a man who has ever played a political game for his own benefit.

"Jordan is attempting to play a mediating role. So much emphasis has been put on the war effort rather than the peace effort. We shall continue to build, instead of trying to destroy.

"My first priority is my husband, because I feel that helping him in any way I can and giving him strength and comfort is also a way of serving the country. He is so important to Jordan because of his efforts. He has great strength and ability and tries to serve his nation as actively and dynamically as possible.

"I try to be a complement to his efforts, a partner. I try to be an extra pair of hands to reach out and touch and find solutions in certain areas so that he does not have to worry about them."

At least conditions were getting better in the refugee camps. "I was devasted when I saw the horrors of the first camps but we've made tremendous progress," the Queen said. "One of our main worries was the spread of disease and the nightmare threat of cholera. But once the rains come in a month or so it will be even more difficult to stop disease. I am told three babies

have died. We still need a great deal of help."

Three Left-wing Labour MPs tried to get in on the peace act. Dennis Canavan, Ron Campbell and Bob Parry hoped to negotiate with Saddam for the release of more British hostages.

Their mission embarrassed Labour leader Neil Kinnnock. One Labour party source said: "If Saddam Hussein can use little boys for propaganda, imagine what he could do with a bunch of MPs." Other Labour MPs thought the trip was "well-intentioned but naive." Tory MPs claimed the stunt was playing straight into the hands of the Iraqi leader. The Liberal Democrats also denounced the move.

The trio were going in a delegation organised by a Malta-based group called the Conference for Peace in the Middle East. The party included Labour Euro MPs and politicians from other nations. The Foreign Office stuck to the expected line by offering the MPs only "normal courtesies" including Gulf crisis briefings.

Before flying out from London Mr Campbell said: "Saddam hasn't got a good track record on human rights. He shoots people. He hangs people. That's a bit of a black mark against him. But I've heard he is very sincere. And he's got a heart."

When the three MPs arrived in Amman Mr Campbell was asked why he had come to see the most powerful Sunni Moslem in the world. He said: "He is a Christian. We're all good Christians. If he is a good man and a Christian he will see us. I am here in the cause of peace, and God says: Thou Shalt Not Kill."

As political gaffes go it was in a league of its

own. They never got to see Saddam anyway. They got as far as the Speaker of the Iraqi Parliament, Sa'ad Mahdi Sadg. He offered to free sick British hostages if members of their families agreed to to take their places.

"I can imagine that if it comes off friends and families would be willing to do a two-week-on, two-week-off rota," said Mr Campbell. "But I doubt if the Government would allow it." He was right about that, at least.

Thousand of Iraqis demonstrated on the streets in Baghdad as President Bush made a TV broadcast to them appealing for peace. The eight-minute videotaped message, handed to Iraqi authorities by US diplomats, blamed Saddam for misleading his countrymen into invading Kuwait. "Iraq stands isolated and alone," President Bush said from the Oval Office. "But it is still possible to bring this crisis to a peaceful end."

Baghdad answered the President's appeal with an instant 20-minute commentary which dissected his words sentence by sentence and explained the Iraqi government's view. The American leader was "a liar who wanted to be dictator of the world".

Saddam warned Americans that they risked another Vietnam by amassing forces in the Middle East. In a right-of-reply TV message to the American people the Iraqi leader insisted: "We do not want war." But he warned that if President Bush started one, Iraq would be powerless to stop it.

"Ladies and gentlemen, Mr Bush is sending your sons to a war which has no human value or meaning save fatal arrogance," he said. And "repeating the Vietnam experience" would lead to consequences "more violent, causing bigger losses."

Pro-Iraqi terror groups again threatened to hit American interests around the world. A statement issued at the end of a conference of Arab political groups in Amman said the first priority was "to strike at American interests everywhere and by all means the moment a U.S. military attack was launched against Iraq".

The three-day conference was called by Arab political parties, guerrilla groups and trade unions. The delegates bitterly attacked the military build-up in the region and those Arab states which had joined the US in opposing Iraq's invasion of Kuwait.

Iraq ordered anyone holding Kuwaiti dinars in the occupied emirate to exchange them for Iraqi currency. Baghdad said that each Kuwaiti dinar, worth $3.50 before the invasion, would be changed for one Iraqi dollar. Iraq's official exchange rate was just over $3.20 to the dinar but outside the country it was actually worth barely a twelfth of that even before the crisis began.

Saddam then repeated his threat to launch missiles against Israel. For the first time since he invaded Kuwait the Iraqi leader warned that he would go on the attack if UN sanctions began to cripple his country. The tone of his warning, backed by intelligence reports which showed Iraqi missile batteries targetted on Israel, alarmed Western diplomats.

Iraq and Israel had no common border. Any Iraqi attack would have to be delivered 200 miles across Jordan. Saddam warned that Israel would be "transformed into something different" and all oilfields in the region destroyed. The statement warned: "Oil, the region and Israel will be the victims of the resulting deluge."

Both the White House and Downing Street feared Israel being drawn into the conflict. A White House source told the Daily Express: "Israel will not sit idly by and let Saddam have his way. They will hit back hard."

Israel was preparing itself for attack. Every village, town and city was on full alert with women and children on stand-by to hide in shelters. Security and civil defence plans were put in force. Every Israeli was issued with a gas mask and drilled in self defence. Iraq was believed to have specially-modified SCUD missiles which had the range to hit cities like Jerusalem or Tel Aviv with chemical warheads.

On the surface, life went on much as usual in Israel. Laughter echoed across Jerusalem's streets as groups of teenagers spilled out of open-air cafes and young couples strolled through the shopping arcades hand-in-hand. In Tel Aviv and Haifa, the main targets for any raid, nightclubs, restaurants and beaches were still packed with people enjoying themselves.

But most families believed that a call to arms for tens of thousands of reservists was only days away. Every home would be affected. All males from 18 to 50 were on stand-by to join up.

Israeli Prime Minister Yitzshak Shamir warned that his nation would hit back at Baghdad "with the most terrible fire". The Iraqi capital was too far for Israeli ground troops to strike and a sneak air attack was impossible – so was this a veiled threat of nuclear retaliation? The Israelis certainly had the hardware. They also had the will to press the button if their existence was threatened.

Iraqis were warned to steel themselves for "the mother of all battles". TV programmes in Baghdad were interrupted for a message from Saddam's Revolution Command Council telling viewers that Iraq would not back off from the Gulf crisis.

"There is not a single chance for any retreat," the statement said although it insisted that Iraq would not fire the first shots. The statement sent world share prices down and oil prices up. Iraqi Information Minister Latif Jassem confirmed that his country would destroy oilfields in the Gulf if it was attacked. "We will respond to aggression with all the weapons at our disposal," he said.

President Bush warned that he would hold Saddam responsible for acts of terrorism against the US. Before going to Camp David for the weekend the President told reporters that his two main concerns were Iraqi's mistreatment of Kuwaitis and possible terrorist attacks by Iraqi agents. "Any such attacks would have serious consequences and I will hold Saddam responsible," he said.

The President refused to rule out military action, whether or not the Iraqis fired the first shot. He said he would also take a grave view if Saddam starved either the hostages or his own people. But he added that war might not be necessary because sanctions were beginning to bite. The US threw out three Iraqi envoys in retaliation for Baghdad's expulsion of American diplomats.

President Bush and Mrs Thatcher held War Cabinets to decide how to enforce an air blockade of Iraq, shortly to be approved by the UN. Their main worry was how not to place civilian aircraft in direct danger. America had already made it clear that civilian aircraft would be "buzzed" to force them to land but they would not be fired on.

Pilots were being warned that if they breached the embargo, their licences could be revoked. Countries backing the blockade would not give any assistance to Iraqi-bound flights which might run into trouble over their territory.

The UN Security Council duly approved the air embargo to back the sea blockade against Iraq. It voted 14-1 to cut off all air traffic to and from Iraq and Kuwait, Cuba alone voting against.

Austria threatened to shoot down any British or US military aircraft flying over its territory in the event of war. American military aircraft on their way to the crisis zone from Germany were, with permission, using Austrian airspace. But Austria, pleading its neutrality, said permission would be withdrawn if hostilities broke out.

Soviet Foreign Minister Eduard Shevardnadze effectively approved the use of force to oust the Iraqis. He said the UN had the power to "suppress acts of aggression" adding: "A great war may break out in the Gulf region any moment."

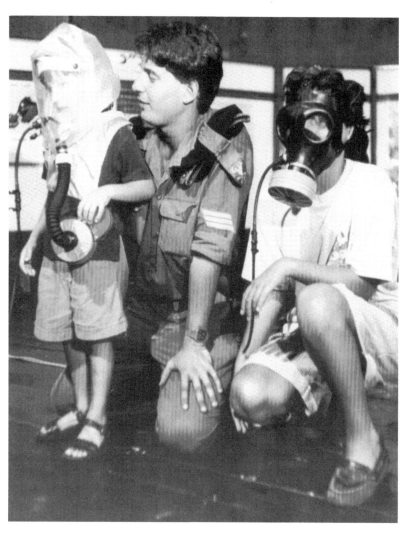

Mrs Thatcher delivered a firebrand speech drawing a direct comparison between the Gulf and the Falklands conflict. "As you go down history, there should be no doubt about what we have to do," she said.

The US Defence Department revealed that Iraq was building up its forces. It now had 430,000 troops in or near Kuwait. There were 3,500 Iraqi tanks and 2,500 armoured personnel carriers in the emirate.

The Desert Rats won a pay pledge from Defence Secretary Tom King, who said they would be £120 a month better off in the Gulf. Chemical warfare suits had been fitted with a new drinking tube enabling servicemen, encouraged to drink gallons of water a day in the desert, to quench their thirsts in their gas masks.

America was told by Iraq that any American refugees found hiding in the US embassy in Baghdad would be hung.

In the days that followed events were to move fast. Britain appointed a new Commander in Chief in the Gulf, Edward Heath announced that he was flying to meet Saddam and the Iraqi leader called for peaceful dialogue to solve the crisis.

The horrifying face of war. Israeli children are shown how to wear gas masks.

CHAPTER 5
THE GULF WAR

'The regime of Saddam Hussein is separated from the civilised world not by space, but by centuries'

George Bush

The elderly shopkeeper stood proudly in front of shelves laden with tinned foods and fresh fruit. Twelve sacks bulging with barley and corn were stacked in the corner.

"Shortage? What shortages?" he shouted as he ushered Expressman Paul Thompson into his Baghdad store. "The people of this city do not go

without. Our women and children will never go hungry."

This was no idle boast, as a tour around the open-air markets and shops confirmed. Two months after trade sanctions were imposed, food was in plentiful supply. Even with the threat of war imminent things continued as normal. Although rationing had been introduced for essential daily items like flour, cooking oil and rice, no family was in desperate need of supplies. According to Western diplomats in Baghdad they were never likely to be no matter how long the embargo lasted.

"The sanctions are just not working and never will," said one envoy. "Large amounts of food are coming in from Jordan. Lebanese traders are making a killing smuggling in supplies."

Thompson toured the Al Sadeer fruit and vegetable market, Baghdad's equivalent of London's New Covent Garden. Behind the ramshackle collection of stalls, teeming with people, were lorries bearing Jordanian number plates.

"Many traders made the gruelling 14-hour drive across harsh desert terrain knowing the rewards were rich," Thompson reported. "But Iraq also had a successful harvest and under a decaying tarpaulin I saw almost every type of vegetable, from huge cauliflowers to runner beans. There was also plenty of fresh fruit on sale.

"Nearby a group of women queued for eggs, while two young housewives stood outside a butcher's shop as he chopped up chunks of beef with a blunt axe. Nearly all the stores were packed with food from Kuwait. Others had boxes with Turkish and Lebanese stamps on them.

"Luxury items never seen before in Baghdad, such as Cadbury's chocolate, Carnation milk and Gentleman's Relish from Fortnum and Mason, were readily available. Such items were likely to stay on the shelves because they were too expensive for the ordinary Iraqi. A jar of honey sold for £15 and a large pack of washing powder was almost £100. With an average monthly wage of £35 few could afford such goods, but their very presence had given the people a new-found confidence."

A British envoy told Thompson: "The West has always used the effectiveness of sanctions in three stages – inconvenience, discomfort and malnutrition. We are still at the inconvenience stage. That is all that rationing means to the Iraqi people. It is not a problem for them. They are prepared for sacrifice and will live on figs and rain water if necessary."

Not a hint of apprehension showed as the people of Baghdad clustered around giant portraits of a smiling Saddam on almost every road junction. For a visiting Westerner like Thompson there was an unreal feeling to a city that was effectively cut off from the rest of the world.

There was no sign of active preparation for war. The impressive six-lane motorways were still full of cars, many of them "liberated" from Kuwait. Young Iraqis cruised up and down in gleaming white Oldsmobiles and upmarket Japanese cars. Monuments to the Iraqi leader dominated the skyline. The people's faith in Saddam was total. Talk of war could not be further from the minds of the couples who walked arm-in- arm along the banks of the Tigris.

Most city centre restaurants had closed after a recent directive from the government, but those in the hotels remained open. Many had actually extended their menus, offering the best fillet steak as meat became more ready available.

"Seeing the hostages or guests, as they are called in Baghdad, walking about freely, lazing by the pool or playing tennis on floodlit courts, belittles the predicament they are in," said Thompson. "I went to to the spacious dining room of one five-star hotel. A group softly played the theme from Love Story while diners enjoyed lavishly- prepared four course meals. The atmosphere was totally relaxed with attentive waiters fussing over the guests.

"One hostage diner remarked, This place is like the Titanic. It's going to go down but the band still plays on."

upplies may have been reaching Baghdad overland but the sea blockade was complete with warships in the Persian Gulf and beyond enforcing the UN embargo.

British forces arrested an Iraqi freighter trying to run the blockade. A helicopter dropped Royal Marine Commandos on to the deck of the Tadmur in the Gulf of Oman. She was carrying rice, flour and other banned cargo. The ship, the first to be caught breaking the UN sanctions against Iraq, was escorted to port. Baghdad denounced the action as "harrassment by sea pirates".

Warships forced another Iraqi ship to stop at the mouth of the Persian Gulf. Three British frigates Battleaxe, London and Adelaide joined the USS Reasoner in firing warning shots across the bows of the Al Wasitti. As the ship slowed to a halt 60 miles off the coast of Muscat, 10 Royal Marines climbed aboard from inflatable power boats. They found no illegal cargo, but the point had been made again.

Already the crisis was costing servicemen's lives. A reconnaisance jet crashed in Saudi Arabia killing two US pilots. Eight other airman in two helicopters were reported missing. Ten sailors were scalded to death in steam on the amphibious assault ship Iwo Jima when a pipe burst in the boiler room. In the Saudi desert a US Marine was killed and three others injured when their pick-up truck overturned. RAF fighter pilot Keith Collister, 26, became the first British serviceman to die in the Gulf when his Jaguar strike jet crashed.

In London a new commander was appointed to lead Britain's desert troops. He was the nation's most-decorated general, Lieutenant-General Sir Peter de la Billiere. The former SAS chief, who masterminded the raid on the Iranian embassy in London and directed the undercover war in the Falklands, was to work hand-in-hand with the American supreme commander of the allied forces.

Sir Peter, 56, had been preparing to retire the following month. "It's so good to be going back," he said after his recall. Appropriately enough, he had served 13 years in Arabia. There were two spells fighting Yemeni-backed Dhofari rebels in Oman, where he won the Military Cross and Bar.

"I would like to think that the Arab way of doing things has rubbed off on me," he said. "One of the personal satisfactions I get out of this appointment is working among Arabs again." He took over from Air Vice Marshal Sandy Wilson.

As Sir Peter's appointment was announced the first British ground forces had arrived in Saudi Arabia. The 285 sappers from the Cambridge-based 39th Engineer Regiment were to build bases for the Desert Rats.

The Rats soon followed. And for the 7,000 men of the 7th Armoured Brigade there were new skills to be learned. Suddenly they were having to pay strict attention to Saudi sensitivities. On the north German plain the upturned sole of an Army boot was unlikely to cause remark, let alone offence, but it was a serious social blunder in the desert where to show an Arab the sole of your shoe is a grave insult.

"Saudi Arabia is our host nation and we want to get on with them, not offend them," Squadron Sgt Major Brian Nicholl, 34, from Northern Ireland told the men.

For the next few days, as tanks and equipment were loaded at the docks, home for the Rats was a sweltering line of grey steel warehouses filled with piles of kitbags and rows of camp beds. Conditions were basic, though there were showers, chemical toilets and food from a field kitchen run by the Americans. The Rats exercised in chemical warfare drills, weapons training, rules of engagement and hygiene and first aid.

Captain Robert Hutton, operations officer for the Queen's Royal Irish Hussars, said: "I'm quite jolly now but at times I go out there and think about it all. I don't think anybody in their right mind wants a war."

Hutton's regiment had already met their American allies. There was much bonhomie and mutual respect. The US Marines, who thrived on their own pride and elitist fighting spirit, had been quick to demonstrate their appreciation of the British Army. Marine Sgt Bill Lowe, a tank commander with the 1st Tank Battalion 1st Marine Expeditionary Force, believed that the British and Americans would work together without a hitch. "All tank crews live exactly the same," he remarked.

One grumble infiltrated the mood of comradeship. Fifty years earlier, during World War II, the Yanks had been "overpaid, over-sexed

'I am a professional soldier... when you are offered a task like this, you do not throw it away freely.'

Sir Peter de la Billiere

COMMANDER WHO LEADS FROM THE FRONT... A REAL SOLDIER'S SOLDIER

Lieutenant-General Sir Peter de la Billiere was Britain's most-decorated general, known to his peers as "a real soldier's soldier". It was no surprise when he was asked to command Britain's forces in the Gulf, except possibly to him.

A keen sailor all his life, he was getting ready to to retire until Mrs Thatcher picked him for command. He had planned to sail with his wife Bridget to Australia on their yacht.

His appointment was a shock, but characteristically he shelved his plans and placed himself at his country's service.

"I have no regrets about not retiring," he said. "I am a professional soldier and when you are offered a task like this you do not throw it away freely."

During his 38 years with the Army, 56-year-old Sir Peter served in Japan, Korea, Egypt, Jordan, Malaysia, Oman, Aden, and Borneo as well as in senior staff appointments in England. He spent 13 of those years in the Gulf, learning what he described as "untidy but workable Arabic".

He joined the SAS in 1956 and later became Commanding Officer. He was then promoted to Commander SAS Group and finally joined the Ministry of Defence as SAS Director.

It was Sir Peter who masterminded the SAS raid on the Iranian Embassy in 1980. During the Falklands war he advised the Prime Minister on covert operations and controlled the SAS campaign.

He was mentioned in despatches after seeing action in Malaya, and then won his first Military Cross for leading his SAS troops under fire in Oman.

One man who was there as he commanded the assault on rebels holding the 10,000 ft Jebel Akhtar mountain said: "He led from the front all the way. That's the way he does things."

Sir Peter was awarded the Bar to his MC for undercover SAS work in Aden in 1965 and after commanding operations in Oman from 1969 to 1974, he was awarded the Distinguished Service Order. His list of honours finally read KCB, CBE, DSO and MC.

His former comrades in the SAS had no doubts about his selection to lead the Gulf force. One said: "He sometimes seems an unlikely general, but he is much shrewder than he lets on.

"He has a quick and brilliant tactical mind and he surrounds himself with people of similar talent. If you don't measure up you are moved pretty damned quick.

"He can be bloody granite, but he is fair and he enjoys a joke. He's a great bloke."

and over here". Nothing changed. They were still paid more than the British soldiers and they had plenty of women in their ranks. The Tommies sighed.

In the desert heat hygiene had become as important as battlefield tactics in preparing for war. Each of the Desert Rats' vehicles was equipped with a portable shower. Squadron Commander Major Hamish MacDonald insisted that his men cooked their own food. It kept them busy and they ran less risk of the stomach upsets which, by now, were plaguing the Americans.

He also made his tank crews spend long hours studying details of what armour Saddam had and how to tell the difference between the Iraqis and the Arab allied forces such as the Egyptians and Syrians.

A blunder was revealed. The Desert Rats still had their jungle camouflage while Iraqi troops sported British-made desert rig. This dated back to the days when Iraq was regarded more favourably by the West. Defence chiefs sold thousands of uniforms to Saddam because they did not think British troops would fight in the desert again. The sold-off uniforms were to the same pattern as those worn during the Aden troubles of the 1960s and the Oman conflict of the 1970s, the last time British troops fought in the Middle East.

"The plan was for the 7th Armoured Brigade and other troops to wear Overseas General, the Army's desert khaki," said a defence analyst. "But when the military went to the central provision department they found it had all gone."

The lack of khaki was being made good fast.

American troops, fortified by 47,000 gallons of Newman's Own Old Fashioned Virginia Lemonade, supplied by the actor Paul Newman, were itching for a fight. They heckled Secretary of State Baker: "Let us do our job or go home!" The challenge was made as Baker began eight days of talks with his military chiefs.

The US decided to replace its main battle tanks in Saudi Arabia to cope with chemical weapons attacks. The tanks on the front line were thought to be vulnerable. So 750 Abrams M1A1 tanks were being shipped to the Gulf from Germany.

On the other side of the Kuwaiti border Saddam was shown inspecting his occupying army. He was pictured standing in a machine gun trench on a beach surrounded by soldiers vowing to die in defence of the annexed emirate. The Iraqi newsagency said Kuwait City "appeared flourishing after its return to the mother homeland".

Then the Israelis handed the dictator a propaganda gift. On October 8 police shot dead 19 Palestinian protestors at Temple Mount in Jerusalem, sparking outrage on all sides.

Saddam promptly vowed to unleash what he called terrifying new missiles on Israel. The Americans feared that he meant missiles with nuclear warheads.

The Iraqi leader warned Israel that they had no choice but to leave the occupied territories or risk annihilation. He said the Temple Mount massacre had pushed the Jewish state "closer to the abyss".

There were also fears that the Iraqis might employ the "supergun" which British Customs thought they had intercepted. British investigators had siezed several key components of the weapon earlier in the year, but a secret Canadian intelligence report suggested that Iraq might have manufactured a prototype. The supergun could hurl a two-ton nerve gas shell into the heart of Jerusalem.

The world condemned the Temple Mount

Life goes on: An American M-1 tank passes a herd of camels on the Saudi sands

'To get out I had to say, loudly I have cancer, I'm dying! Now I am going back to saying I am cured! I am an eternal optimist. And Ted Heath is magic.'

*freed hostage
Tony Wilbraham*

killings but the government of hardliner Yitzak Shamir warned that it would not co-operate with a UN investigative commission into the shootings. Shamir was reported to be "hopping mad" at what he saw as a largely British-engineered Security Council resolution heavily critical of Israel. Douglas Hurd fuelled his anger by twice condemning the Israeli action as "reckless and misplaced." He also made it clear that Israel would be "unwise" to refuse the UN mission.

Israel saw Mr Hurd's repeated condemnations as direct interference in its internal affairs. Israeli foreign minister David Levy said to accept the UN delegation "would be to accept that Jerusalem is not our legal capital".

The row died down as the world turned back to the real issue, the Gulf crisis. Britain sent 5,000 more troops and another 60 Challenger tanks. US Defence Secretary Dick Cheney authorised the Pentagon to call up 72,500 more reservists.

Saddam announced that he would start freeing all foreign hostages as "a gesture of goodwill".

In the desert, Western fighter jets streaked low across the dunes in sight of Iraqi tanks as the allied forces staged a mock invasion of Kuwait. Stealth bombers teased and probed the Iraqi air defences at awesome speeds. American commanders insisted that it was just an exercise, but the sight of 1,100 strike planes darkening the sky as they swarmed in, during the subtly-titled Operation Imminent Thunder, must have made the battle-hardened Iraqi troops reflect on what might come.

The hostages continued to make news. One touching story was told in a one-page letter to nurse Helen Sykes, 25. She had been worrying for weeks over the fate of her boyfriend, hotel reception manager Mark Eggington, 30, held in Baghdad. She had not heard from him since she fled from Kuwait at the start of the crisis. It was believed to be the first letter from a hostage to get through. Mark wrote:

"I hope you get this because it means you are safe and well and back with your family. I'm sorry for the heartache I have caused to both you and the family for failing in my duty to protect you."

He also apologised for not being able to give details of where he was being held captive. The Iraqis censored everything. He was fit and well, he added, though he had lost weight.

Helen said at her home in South Yorkshire: "I was working in a hotel out there when it all flared up. I managed to get to Baghdad and then a flight to Jordan. But I had no way of knowing what had happened to Mark. I have been writing letters on

a weekly basis and I still do not know if they are getting through. Even though Mark's letter took 20 days to reach me I was elated when I read it and discovered that he was all right."

A political row over the hostages exploded when former Tory leader Edward Heath announced that he would be flying to Baghdad to seek the release of up to 200 captives, most of them old or sick or both.

He revealed his trip during the Tory conference in Bournemouth to the fury of some of his colleagues, who saw it as an attempt to upstage the Prime Minister's speech and, at the same time, hand Saddam a propaganda victory. "Mrs Thatcher has made it clear time and again that there will be no negotiations over the hostages," said one senior party source. "They must be released unconditionally and not bargained over."

Mr Heath, 74, retorted that he was responding to requests from the hostages' families. He could not live with himself if he did not do something to try to help, he said.

"I have thought long and seriously about this and I have decided to go to Amman and Baghdad," Mr Heath announced. "I am told I will be welcome. President Saddam is expecting me and a discussion has been arranged. I cannot say what the outcome will be. The purpose of my visit is to help the sick and dying, nothing else.

"I accept that I will be criticised by the Government and the party but I do not think I am going to be criticised by the relatives of those trapped in the Middle East."

A friend added: "Some believe that he has timed the announcement of a visit to Iraq as a publicity stunt in a bid to upstage Mrs Thatcher's speech to the conference. They could not be more wrong. He just wants to do all he can to help the hostages."

The row was compounded when Mr Heath claimed on TV that Douglas Hurd had asked him to approach Saddam on behalf of the hostages in Iraq. Mr Hurd, then in Cairo, admitted discussing it on the phone with Mr Heath but denied that he asked the former Prime Minister to intervene.

"I did NOT ask Mr Heath to go," he said. "Mr Heath had been approached for help by a relative of a Briton, seriously ill in Baghdad. It was suggested that I ring Mr Heath to discuss it, since he had not made up his mind. I did so and handled the matter very carefully. I neither encouraged nor discouraged him. The Prime Minister was kept informed and there was no objection."

Mr Heath told David Frost on TV-am that the mission was entirely Mr Hurd's idea. "I had to think about it but I finally said Yes, I would be prepared to go," he said.

**Hostage hope: Former
Tory Prime Minister Ted
Heath negotiates the
release of trapped
Britons with Saddam**

And go he did, returning aboard Richard Branson's Scarlet Lady flagship jumbo with 38 freed hostages on October 24. They drank a champagne toast to the former Tory leader as cabin staff cheered.

"Now I'll either rip up my passport or frame it," said the oldest hostage, 70-year-old Scottish pensioner Mary Wright. "It was my first and last trip abroad."

Her husband Jim, 69, a stroke victim, added: "I've been fiddling with the keys to our home all this time. Now I'll be opening our front door again."

Mr Heath was disappointed in having to settle for only 38 hostages. He had hoped for as many as 200 and the British Embassy in Baghdad had drawn up a list of 53 sick, injured and elderly people it regarded as priority cases. Some were told they could go home only to be stopped from leaving at the last minute. They gamely shook hands with the lucky ones and wished them well.

Two of Saddam's British hostages would never be coming home. One was brilliant 19-year-old Oxford University student Alexander Duncan, killed in a car crash on his way to join Mr Heath's flight. His brother Rory, 18, was seriously injured. Another was engineer Ron Duffy, 62, who collapsed and died of a heart attack at a military compound outside Baghdad. "He never had a day's illness before," wept his widow Christine in Newcastle upon Tyne. "No other family should have to go through what we have had to endure."

Of course there was joy too. Cancer victim Tony Wilbraham said: "To get out I had to say, loudly I have cancer, I'm dying! Now I am going back to saying I am cured! I am an eternal optimist. And Ted Heath is magic."

The freed hostages told their by-now familiar tales of captivity. Banker Colin McGregor, 50,

said he had been held in a factory for seven weeks and banned from going outside. "We were not even allowed to look out," he said. "They even covered the fence with cardboard so we couldn't see through it."

Another hostage told how a 59-year-old Briton was still hiding out in Kuwait City in a dark, 10ft by 6ft cubbyhole he had built under a stairway in an otherwise deserted apartment. The Briton, an engineer, had walled off the space himself and painted the partitions the same colour as the surrounding walls. There was one tiny opening, closed off by a concealed door on wheels. The fugitive was living on biscuits, tinned food and bottled water, constantly listening out for the footsteps of Iraqi soldiers. He crept out at night the most dangerous time, during the hours of curfew, to dump his rubbish.

Another homecoming expatriate was 25-year-old computer engineer Derek MacGowan. He made it under his own steam, driving through the desert dodging Iraqi troops, but he could not dodge British Customs at Gatwick. Derek was held for two hours, fined £115 and ordered to pay £127 tax for not declaring a video camera. He complained to his MP, who complained to Mrs Thatcher, who waived the fine but not the tax.

Back in Baghdad, 14 American hostages were put on a flight to Jordan and Iraq's parliament rubber-stamped a Saddam proposal to release all his 330 French hostages. The French welcomed the news but President Mitterrand still stuck by the UN resolutions demanding Iraq's withdrawal from Kuwait and the release of all hostages.

Saddam told the Soviets that their 5,000 nationals still in Iraq would be held hostage if they gave any war secrets to the US. "We warn Moscow against such behaviour," said a spokesman. The Kremlin had been Saddam's

'During the last war, we never heard sobs from widows. Why can't these people keep a stiff upper lip?'

Sir John Stokes

chief arms supplier but the KGB had already said it may share its intelligence with the CIA.

In Britain wives of the British hostages angrily condemned Tory MP Sir John Stokes, 73, who had told them to stop bleating. "During the last war we never heard sobs from widows," he said. "Why can't these people keep a stiff upper lip and think of the country as a whole instead of their own personal concerns? I am sick and tired of the mewling and puking of the relatives of hostages in the Gulf and of some of the hostages themselves."

The Gulf Support Group said: "His comments are really beneath contempt." Mrs Dorothy Goodwin, one of a group of wives planning to fly to Baghdad to visit their hostage husbands, said: "We are not mewling, weeping women. We are going to Baghdad with dignity and respect. I would like to know if Sir John has any relatives in Iraq. If he hasn't, then I don't think his remarks are very constructive."

British Telecom bowed to pressure and agreed to cut its charges for families ringing hostages in Baghdad. Saddam had blocked direct-dialling facilities from Britain, meaning that callers had to go through the operator. The direct-dialling charges had been £11.49 for 10 minutes cheap rate, £13.51 standard rate. Calls through the operator cost £26.45. MPs protested and Telecom chairman Iain Vallance agreed to go back to the old rates.

For ordinary Britons the immediate effect of the Gulf crisis was the rocketing price of petrol. Former Saudi oil minister Sheikh Yamani warned that there was a 50-50 chance of a war which could triple crude prices to $100 a barrel.

In the UK an independent watchdog to monitor forecourt costs was being set up. Daily checks were to be made on pump prices to see if the oil giants were profiteering. The scheme was devised by filling station owners and managers, who had borne the brunt of drivers' anger as prices spiralled. There was concern that once the crisis was over the oil companies would take advantage of the situation to keep charges high.

Elsewhere the jaw-jaw went on-on. Saddam called for peace talks instead of threats to resolve the crisis and withdrew his opposition to the involvement of foreign powers in the search for a settlement. Saddam adopted his softer stance in a TV message marking the birthday of the Prophet Mohammed. Foreign countries could help solve the crisis, he said, "if the language of peaceful politics replaces the policy of troop build-ups and threats of force".

But he stressed that his army would not be

recalled from Kuwait until certain conditions were met. He linked any settlement to an Israeli withdrawal from the occupied West Bank and Gaza and the pull-out of Syrian forces from Lebanon. Saddam also called for talks with France, favouring President Mitterrand's ideas on the conflict. Mitterrand had suggested that the Gulf crisis and the other problems in the region could be settled together. Saddam's pleas were dismissed by the Foreign Office as nothing new.

Mrs Thatcher, in New York, unveiled plans to make Iraq pay crippling reparations for its invasion of Kuwait. The Prime Minister was ready to sponsor a new UN Security Council resolution demanding that Iraqi assets in the West be frozen. Billions of dollars were involved which should be used to compensate the ousted Emir of Kuwait and his people, she said. Mrs Thatcher still insisted that Saddam face a war crimes tribunal.

She met the Emir of Kuwait and pledged that British troops would remain in Kuwait after Saddam had been driven out. President Bush had already told the Saudis that Operation Desert Shield would remain in place for as long as they needed it.

The Emir told Mrs Thatcher that the Iraqis had been executing Kuwaiti resistance fighters in front of their families. Amnesty International confirmed the executions and reported that Iraqi troops were also torturing captives. Saddam denied the charges.

President Bush, again condemned the Iraqi invasion, drawing parallels with Hitler's march into Poland in 1939. And citing the eight UN resolutions condemning Saddam's aggression he said: "Today the regime stands isolated and out of step with the times, separated from the civilised world not by space, but by centuries."

Iraq surprised the West by offering to sell its oil at knockdown prices even to the US. Saddam was apparently prepared to offload his country's vast stocks more cheaply than any other nation to raise cash. The Iraqi leader even offered a buy-now-pay-later deal. He said he would sell the oil at $21 a barrel when the market price was then $34 a barrel. His offer was not taken up.

President Bush confirmed that he was sending Secretary of State Baker to Saudi Arabia to get King Fahd's permission to launch an attack on Saddam if it was "deemed necessary" by the White House. The Pentagon hinted that a further 250,000 US troops could be sent to the desert in addition to the 220,000 already there.

On October 29, the UN Security Council voted to hold Iraq legally accountable for war damages. The move meant that Saddam faced a bill for billions from countries, firms and individuals

Blast off: Space shuttle Atlantis heads skywards from Cape Canaveral on a spy mission over Iraq

over his invasion. The UN urged Iraq's opponents to compile dossiers detailing any outrages, paving the way for the prosecution of Iraqis for war crimes. The Security Council also called on Iraq to restore water, electricity and food supplies to the besieged foreign embassies in Kuwait City. The resolution was approved 13 to 0 with Cuba and Yemen abstaining.

Western reporters clamoured to get into Kuwait. Iraq's deputy prime minister, Taha Ramadam, told them: "It is an Iraqi province and we will chop the legs off anyone who enters illegally."

In Britain, Labour MPs Bernie Grant, Ron Brown and Tony Benn planned peace missions to Baghdad. Cardinal Basil Hume, leader of the country's Roman Catholics, gave his conditional backing to war in the Gulf and petrol prices began to fall with Texaco cutting 4p off a gallon of four-star. The Space Shuttle Atlantis lifted off from Cape Canaveral on a secret mission that was expected to place a spy satellite over Iraq. Thousands of American tourists stayed away from Britain fearing an Iraqi- sponsored campaign of terror and Germany's Helmut Kohl sanctioned a peace mission to Baghdad to free hostages by veteran stateman Willy Brandt.

Saddam, in an interview with ITN's Trevor McDonald in Baghdad, denied that his troops had committed atrocities in occupied Kuwait. He also denied that the hostages were prisoners. Saddam refused to give any hint that he might withdraw from Kuwait but stressed the importance of dialogue to resolve the crisis. He insisted Iraq had justice on its side and complained of a Western conspiracy against him.

Foreign Secretary Douglas Hurd, speaking in Cairo, warned Saddam that if he did not quit Kuwait peacefully he would do so "at the point of a gun."

Iraq's official newsagency ridiculed the threat. "If Hurd thinks his language scares anyone he is deceiving himself," it said. Britain had enslaved people when it had colonies, the agency went on, and repeated Saddam's claim that Britain had separated Kuwait from Iraq when it colonised the Gulf earlier this century. "The Iraqis have destroyed forever the filthy British scissors with which the ancestors of Hurd and old hag Thatcher had cut off a dear part of Iraq."

Saddam warned that Western leaders would be to blame if any Iraqi children died of lack of food or medicine. He attacked Mrs Thatcher and President Bush for being behind the UN embargo. "Those who shed crocodile tears for children dying in the world are responsible for these tragedies," he said in a speech marking Iraqi Children's Day.

Tempers were short, and getting shorter. President Bush let his frustration with Saddam rip. In an emotional appeal to American patriotism he told a political rally: "The American flag is flying over the Kuwait embassy and our people inside are being starved by a brutal dictator. Do you think I am concerned about that? Your darned right I am. What am I going to do about it? Just wait and see. Because I've had it with that kind of treatment of Americans. And I know that Margaret Thatcher feels the same way about the Brits."

She did. But to the president's consternation, she was not to remain at Number 10 for long.

CHAPTER 6

THE GULF WAR

'If Saddam Hussein remains in Kuwait, which is like a prison camp, and which he is dismantling day by day, he will have to be forcibly removed. No one wants a war. But the person who can stop it . . . is Saddam'

John Major

"It's a funny old world," Mrs Thatcher told her colleagues around the Cabinet table at Number 10 Downing Street. Then she burst into tears. The Thatcher years were over.

The Iron Lady had only barely beaten off a leadership challenge from Tory MP Michael Heseltine. Her natural instinct was to fight on and on but a series of Tory party functionaries, the famous Men in Grey Suits, warned her to quit or face a humiliating defeat. She quit. Heseltine withdrew from the race "in the interests of national unity" and Britain had a new Prime Minister, former Chancellor John Major.

A White House aide said President Bush was stunned by Mrs Thatcher's resignation. "It hurt him deeply," the aide said. The President tried to reach her from Saudi Arabia, attempting to telephone London from his helicopter at one

point. When he did get through he told the Prime Minister: "Maggie, we love you." Later he said publicly: "I think everybody in America would agree that she has been an outstanding ally for the United States."

Former President Ronald Reagan said: "As she has done throughout her career, Margaret Thatcher has made a selfless and courageous decision in what she believes is the best interest of her country."

In Moscow, where Pravda had given her the Iron Lady tag, they described her as the woman who had discovered Mikhail Gorbachev for the West. Gorbachev himself said her decision to go was a courageous choice made by a courageous politician. "Such a political leader leaves bright pages not only in the history of her country but in the history of the world," the Soviet president's spokesman added.

Common Market president Jacques Delors, who had had his share of clashes with Mrs Thatcher over the future of Europe, said: "I held her in high esteem."

Israel's premier Yitzhak Shamir said: "I feel great sadness in my heart."

Mrs Thatcher's redoubtable husband Denis was more forthright. "Stuff 'em!" he told her. "You have been beaten by idiots in your own party." On the day she announced her resignation he repeated to fellow lunchers at the Savoy: "She wasn't beaten by Labour or Heseltine, she was beaten by idiots in her own party." Then he marched along the Strand and down Whitehall back to Downing Street.

Daughter Carole told her mother: "Mum, there should be a new four-letter swear word in the English language Tory." Son Mark matched his father's anger on an echoeing satellite link from Dallas and blasted the MPs who he believed had betrayed his mother. He had only just arrived in Dallas from a London visit but he caught the first British Airways flight back to Heathrow.

Mr Major, 47, was quick to reassure the Allies that there would be no change in Britain's stance on the Gulf. One of Mrs Thatcher's last acts had been to announce that another 14,000 troops would be going to the Middle East, and that stood.

For over a decade Americans had seen Mrs Thatcher as their favourite sometimes, seemingly, only European ally. When Mr Major arrived in the US just before Christmas to a low-key welcome there were fears that he would compare unfavourably with Mrs Thatcher's heavyweight presence. There was a shaky start when one TV network kept getting his name wrong, insisting on calling him John Majors.

But after a "getting to know you" session with President Bush at Camp David, the Americans were soon hailing Mr Major as the natural successor to Mrs Thatcher. In a whirlwind round of breakfast TV interviews, journalists plugged away at him over the Gulf crisis. He impressed the Americans when he repeated that there would no change in Britain's stand, and refused to give house room to American calls for a compromise if Saddam withdrew from most of Kuwait.

"If he remains in Kuwait, which is like a prison camp and which he is dismantling day by day, he will have to be forcibly removed," Mr Major said. "A partial withdrawal will not do."

There was a principle at stake, he argued. If Saddam was allowed to remain in Kuwait other small countries would feel threatened by their bigger neighbours.

And he added: "If Saddam thinks the West is not serious he might ask himself why the US has

400,000 troops and the UK nearly 40,000 in the Gulf. No one wants a war if it can be stopped. But the person who can stop it is Saddam."

President Bush had offered to "go that last mile for peace". He had invited Iraq's foreign minister, Tariq Aziz, to Washington and offered to send Secretary of State Baker to Baghdad. The move came 24 hours after the UN Security Council, on a Soviet initiative, gave Saddam an ultimatum to get out of Kuwait or face military action. The deadline was set for midnight, New York time, on January 15 1991. The vote was 12 in favour with Cuba and Yemen opposed and China abstaining.

Tens of thousands of Iraqis took to the streets of Baghdad to protest against the resolution. The Pentagon announced that another 20,000 GIs and another 300 warplanes were on their way to the Gulf. The Soviet Union warned Iraq that it would not hesitate to use force to protect its 3,300 citizens still in the country.

President Bush, in a televised address to the American people, said: "Let me assure you that if military action is required this will not be a protracted, drawn-out war. I promise you that there will not be a murky ending. If one American soldier goes into battle that soldier will have enough force behind him to win and to get out."

But there was a sigh of relief around the world when President Bush's offer of peace talks was welcomed by Iraq's ambassador in Paris, Abdul Razzak al-Hashimi, who said: "This is a very important step." The next day the best hope of a peaceful settlement to the crisis came as Iraq accepted President Bush's offer of talks. The country's 11-man Revolutionary General Command, headed by Saddam, met in emergency session and decided to take the olive branch.

However it quickly became clear that Iraq would want to centre any negotiations on wider Middle Eastern issues. In an interview with the Sunday Express the Iraqi ambassador to Britain, Dr Azmi al-Salihi, stressed that talks would have to include attempts to find a solution to the Palestinian problem as well as the Israeli occupation of the West Bank.

President Bush dismissed the idea. "Saddam needs to get out of Kuwait without trying to complicate this matter by talking about some Middle East peace settlement or conference."

Saddam then proceeded to reject 15 suggested dates for a meeting with James Baker. Speaking on the White House lawn, on December 15, President Bush said America had given the dates, all before January 3, and Saddam had given only one, January 12, three days before the deadline.

"In offering to go an extra mile for peace I did not offer to be a party to Saddam's manipulation,"

the President declared. "He is not too busy to see at short notice Kurt Waldheim, Willy Brandt, Mohammed Ali, Ted Heath and many others. It simply is not credible that he could not make a couple of hours available for the Secretary of State."

Saddam told German TV: "Allah is on our side that is why we will beat the aggressor." He predicted great losses if the Allied forces went to war, "not just in terms of human life. Those who now say Yes to war will be responsible." The Iraqi leader accused the US of aiming to conquer the holy places of Islam and added: "We say to Bush Leave our country. If there are problems among the Arabs, they can solve them."

Other Arab leaders painted a nightmare picture of hundreds of thousands dying in a war. The apocalyptic warnings came from Egyptian president Hosni Mubarak and Saudi Arabia's King Fahd. Mubarak, who had 40,000 troops in the 28-nation force opposing Saddam, mostly on the Iraqi border, said in Cairo: "The decision of one man will lead to the deaths of hundreds of thousands." Fahd told a meeting of five Gulf neighbours that a disastrous war would be entirely Iraq's fault...and that Saddam's own people would be the first victims.

Iraq caught an increasingly pessimistic world on the hop by suddenly announcing the immediate release of all human shield hostages. It looked as though they would be home for Christmas. The champagne corks popped all over Britain.

Young Stuart Lockwood, who had been pawed by Saddam on TV and had since become a symbol for the innocents caught in the crisis, was summoned from his school classroom. It was his mother on the phone. "Your father will soon be free," she said.

Mrs Glenda Lockwood told reporters: "Now we are just praying it all comes true and my husband will be back in my arms soon. All my boys want for Christmas is their daddy. God, what will I do if it all goes wrong? I will have to bring them back to earth. Craig, our eldest, has been quite adult from the start and has dealt well with the situation, trying to stand in while daddy is away. But Stuart, well, I'm just praying."

There were shrieks of joy at the Gulf Support Group HQ in London as relatives celebrated the news that their loved ones could be home in time for Christmas. Within minutes of Saddam's announcement, excited families jammed the switchboard, eager to hear more details and swap messages of congratulation. Others turned up at the door and hugged each other in relief.

"I've been in tears since I heard the news," said

Linda Grant, 43, whose 46-year-old husband Roy was being held in Baghdad and had not seen his newborn grandson yet. "If Saddam was here at this minute I would kiss him. God, please let it be true. Roy is a survivor but I expect his reaction will be the same as mine – floods of tears."

Words of caution came through the euphoria. Britain's ambassador in Baghdad, Harold Walker, said: "I have one grey and boring reservation. People should believe their exit visas when they see them."

Support group founder member Joanna Copley said: "We still have to be careful. It is difficult for Saddam to backtrack now but it is important that nobody, no politician anywhere, says anything that may jeopardise the release of these people. They have been waiting for four months. We need them home."

John Major welcomed the news. "I will be even happier when they are back in the country," he added. The Prime Minister warned that Saddam had still not done enough to lift the threat of war. "He still has to withdraw totally and unconditionally from Kuwait and the legitimate government must be restored," he said.

Foreign Secretary Douglas Hurd told the Commons: "We have 440 British nationals in hiding in Kuwait. We have 355 nationals at liberty in Iraq and a further 342 detained at strategic sites. That is just about 1,150 all told."

Saddam was no hero for releasing people who should never have been taken hostage in the first place, he pointed out.

The Foreign Office officially advised hideaway hostages in Kuwait over the BBC World Service that it was safe to come out into the open. Slowly, nervously, hundreds of men broke cover for the first time since August and took their first steps to freedom. They emerged from their hiding places and edged on to the dusty, deserted streets, heading for an agreed rendezvous point. Some were not ashamed to cry as they said their goodbyes to Kuwaiti friends who had helped them and who now faced an uncertain future. Volunteer wardens helped them into waiting cars and vans and drove them to Kuwait Aiport, past sandbagged machine gun nests dug in around the abandoned government buildings.

A little after 7am the first hostages began milling around the Iraqi Airlines desk in the once-ornate airport terminal building, now stripped of its chandeliers and plate glass. Everyone wanted to believe that their ordeal was ending, but no one dared to relax. Only once did the Britons cheer, when two green and white Iraqi Airways Boeing 707s dipped out of the hazy sky. They were on their way home.

More than 100 British hostages arrived on a

champagne flight to Heathrow on the morning of December 10. Wives and children embraced the men they feared they would never see again. The families had struggled through sleet and ice all over freezing Britain to say welcome home. One freed hostage held his baby son and told him: "I'm never going to put you down."

The hostages again brought back stories of their life in hiding or in captivity.

David Dorrington twice had to hide from Iraqi soldiers in a tiny cavity in his bathroom ceiling. The 43-year-banker, from Chingford, spent four months in a house in Kuwait with five other Britons. "The worst thing about being out there was the knock on the door," he said. "Any moment soldiers with guns could have taken us away."

David and his fellow fugitives relied on local Kuwaitis for food. "They were risking their lives to help us," he said. "They could have been shot."

Human shield hostage Edward May had been held captive on the campus of Kuwait University, sharing a four-bedroomed house with six other

It's over: The feeling of freedom is shown to the world by released hostage David Dorrington and his wife Susan at Heathrow Airport

'Kuwait was devastated. There was looting and mindless vandalism. Street after street was in tatters. We grabbed our bikes and headed back to the airport'

Captain Richard Bunyate

men. He passed the time writing short stories and keeping a diary on his computer.

"We managed on a daily diet of bread and watery soup," he said. "In the evenings we had rice and what we could only describe as slops."

Then he was taken to Iraq and held at a strategic chemicals factory. "We had no trouble from the Iraqi guards," he revealed. "They were more frightened of us than we were of them. But I am looking forward to a walk in the green fields of Kent and being able to stroll without a man saying: Mister, you can't go there.' And without a man with a Kalashnikov telling me what I can or cannot do. When I got off the plane I was euphoric. I have been holding my emotions in check for months but now I feel great."

His wife Sue, there to meet him, said: "I thought at times I might never see him again."

Other freedom flights rolled in during the following days, all bringing Britons telling of life in Kuwait and Iraq. British Airways pilot Richard Bunyate, 42, revealed how he had cycled to freedom after 100 days on the run.

Richard, his crew and their passengers had been stranded on the tarmac at Kuwait in their Boeing 747 Coniston Water on the morning of the invasion. The Iraqis rounded them up at gunpoint and interned them in Kuwait's Regency Hotel for a fortnight. After placing his passengers with their embassies, Richard and his crew began to think of their own escape.

In the event, they had just five minutes to make a break for it before troops arrived to escort them to Baghdad. Richard led his two stewardesses and three flight crew into the darkened streets.

"I had been looking for likely hiding holes, going out dressed in Arab robes to avoid detection," he said. "When it came to D-Day I had little time. The six of us fled the Regency and went to the home of a great little guy. Like everyone who helped us he was brave, frightened and someone I will always remember.

"We went from one safe house to another, living on lentils and scraps of meat. At first we thought we had blown the girls' chances of getting home when the 'women-only' release was announced, but we got them out. They were flown to Britain while we carried on moving around the suburbs with the Resistance.

"Kuwait was devastated. There was looting and mindless vandalism. Street after street was in tatters. We kept hearing the rattle of gunfire and the rumble of tanks but we saw no fighting. We stayed one step ahead and survived.

"Finally we thought enough was enough when we heard the 'Come Out' message from the BBC. We still suspected the Iraqis, so we waited 24 hours. Then we took our bikes and rode to the

airport to get a flight.

"Coming aboard the final BA flight home and seeing all my colleagues again was one hell of an experience. I felt really small when the whole plane burst into spontaneous applause. Now just looking at my family brings a lump to my throat."

His wife Carol said: "I knew Richard would make it. And I'm so proud of him for helping others."

A tough sergeant major fought back tears of rage when he told how Iraqi troops had assaulted his wife and kissed a neighbour's SON. Michael Haynes, 37, had been in Kuwait with other service personnel advising the Kuwaiti military and was not home when it happened.

"The Iraqi soldiers kicked down my kitchen door, came into the house and attacked my wife Elaine and her friend," he said. "They placed their hands under the women's clothing, held my five-year-old son with a knife at his throat and robbed my wife of her engagement ring and necklace.

"They also attacked the children of the other family in our house. The young boy had his gold chain and watch removed and then the Iraqis kissed him. It was disgusting."

The return of the hostages was a bitter-sweet story for Gloria Byng, 47. Her brother Don Major, 57, died from a heart attack in captivity. The tragedy prompted her to write to the Prime Minister protesting about what she saw as the Government's inaction over the hostages.

"It's just very, very sad that freedom came too late for Don," said Mrs Byng, of Portsmouth. "Unfortunately the release does not make my family feel any better about our loss. In a way it makes it worse. But just because Saddam is freeing all the hostages does not mean there isn't going to be a war. All our prayers now should be for the service personnel in the desert."

Finally, little Stuart Lockwood raced across the tarmac at Gatwick and threw his arms around his father Derek. "Daddy, it's great to have you back," he said. "Now all I want for Christmas is a train set."

Derek grinned: "This is the most wonderful moment of my life."

Stuart got his train set, and more besides. He was rewarded for his courage in standing up to Saddam with a bravery commendation from the Duchess of York, who told him he had a trendy haircut and let him sit in her Bentley. Stuart fingered his enamel Children of Courage badge and said: "Saddam Hussein has got loads of medals but not as nice as this one. This is a lot more fun than meeting Saddam. The Bentley car has a telephone and seats that tip up where the detectives sit."

The fugitives who fled Kuwait left behind a country on the rack. Amnesty International published a chilling 80-page catalogue of atrocities perpetrated by the invaders.

The Iraqis had murdered 300 babies, according to Amnesty. The youngest victims were premature babies who died when troops seized incubators from three Kuwaiti hospitals.

The investigators listed 38 forms of torture used by the military, including beatings, the rape of both women and men, castration, the gouging-out of eyes and electric shocks. Some victims were blinded by having cigarettes stubbed out in their eyes. Fingernails were torn out, tongues and ears cut off and holes bored in people's legs.

"Reports of violations continue to reach us almost daily," Amnesty said. Its findings were sent to the UN. Britain's ambassador to Iraq, 58-year-old Harold Walker, said: "The things that have been in Kuwait by Iraqis are appalling. They have brought disgrace on their country." Mr Walker was speaking in London after arriving on a flight with 13 freed hostages.

Britain's two top men in Kuwait left the country after 16 weeks trapped in their embassy. Ambassador Michael Weston and consul Larry Banks travelled to Jordan after climbing down a ladder from the first floor to leave the building locked. They had been ordered home by the Government, but Mr Weston did not want to leave. "I wanted to stay until the legitimate government of Kuwait was restored," he said.

The Foreign Office advised thousand of British women and children living in the northern half of the Gulf within range of Iraqi chemical weapons to leave before January 15. About 10,500 dependants including 4,235 children were in the region covered by the warning. It took in families in Bahrain, Qatar, Eastern Saudi Arabia, Riyadh and Tabuk.

The Allied troop build-up continued remorselessly. Commanders constantly exercised their men as much to stave off boredom as to prepare them for combat. Saudi Arabia was a land with no bars, no cinemas, no available women.

And definitely no knees. Service censors had the job of going through every copy of the Daily Express entering the kingdom, blacking out the kneecaps of every girl pictured in the paper. The same went for the slightest hint of cleavage and any ads for alcohol. The felt-tip fusiliers went through every publication coming in, one by one.

There had been problems with the Saudis. When the RAF Regiment raised the Union Jack they were ordered to take it down, at first. The Americans refused to paint out the red crosses on

their ambulances after the Saudis claimed they were a symbol of the Crusades. Arabs screamed at the women soldiers to cover up.

The founder of modern Saudi Arabia, Ibn Saud, had said: "My kingdom will survive only insofar as it remains a country difficult of access, where the foreigner will have no other aim, with his task fulfilled, but to get out." His words still went for most Saudis. If it caused resentment among the Western troops who were putting their lives on the line to preserve the country, they were too well-disciplined to show it.

America revealed that it was chartering a ship to provide R&R for its forces. The White House was paying more than £16 million to hire the Cunard cruise liner Princess. Up to 800 troops at a time would be able to drink and dance with their female colleagues, watch movies, swim and lie around in Jacuzzis as the Princess cruised up and down outside Saudi territorial waters.

No such fun afloat for the British Tommies. Their main recreation was the imaginative maltreatment of Army rations. One concoction, known as the all-inner, was a mixture of half a dozen tins of anything that came to hand. Expressman Danny McGrory dined with the artillery.

"The feast comprised beef stew, mulligatawny soup, baked beans and sliced peaches all slopped

Child of courage: Fergie pays tribute to boy hostage Stuart Lockwood

into a mess tin and heated," he reported. "It tastes better than it looks, but the real beauty is that it saves on the washing up.

"For all their jibes the gourmet gunners have few complaints about Army rations. But they would like whoever in Whitehall packs their compo' to know that they never want to see another tin of pilchards again. Gold tins of the offending fish litter the desert, all that is ever left from the 10-man ration packs they devour."

"By comparison the Americans are almost mutinous over the state of their rations, known as MREs, or Meals Ready to Eat. They are more tastelessly known as Meals Rejected by Ethiopians."

Three tons of teabags, enough to fill a double-decker bus, were flown out by the Tea Council after the Desert Rats pleaded for a decent cuppa. They had enough now for two million.

A massive reinforcement for British troops arrived. Veteran comic Harry Secombe, himself a Desert Rat during World War II who saw action in North Africa and Sicily, told the soldiers in the Saudi desert that his war cry had been: "Help! Run for your lives!" He added: "I was in the Army leading retreats."

The GIs were promised 87-year-old Bob Hope but denied actress Brooke Shields, who had been on the point of flying out to the desert when the Saudis turned down her entry visa because she was "a young, single, female entertainer".

Rambo actor Sylvester Stallone angered many when he turned down an invitation to visit the US Marines in the Gulf because he disagreed with a conflict that risked a single American life. In a TV interview he said that if the US had no other option it should launch a nuclear strike against Baghdad. "That way no Americans would get hurt," Stallone said.

American and British leaders embarked on morale-boosting tours of the troops.

President Bush was in Saudi Arabia for Thanksgiving. Dressed in combat jacket, blue open-neck shirt and fawn slacks he punched the air and said: "Saddam's invasion of Kuwait simply will not stand. We will not pull our punches. We are confronting a bully who thinks he can get away with kicking sand in the face of the world. So far we have acted with restraint, as is our way. But Saddam is making the mistake of confusing an abundance of restraint and patience with lack of resolve. Every day that passes brings Saddam Hussein one step closer to realising his goal of a nuclear weapons arsenal and that's another reason why more and more our mission is marked by a real sense of urgency."

His commander-in-chief in the Gulf, General Stormin' Norman Schwarzkopf, said Saddam's troops were positioned for a tough defensive land battle. He predicted that all-out war could last six months. And he warned: "It's not the size of the dog in the fight, it's the size of fight in the dog."

American Defence Secretary Dick Cheney arrived in the Gulf with more sombre news. He feared that war with Iraq was getting more likely every day. "It looks increasingly like Saddam is not getting the message and we will have to use

SCHWARZKOPF: 'A SOLDIER YOU WOULDN'T MIND SHARING A FOXHOLE WITH'

Wherever the larger-than-life figure of four-star General Stormin' Norman Schwarzkopf went, his home went with him. He had a heart, and next to it he carried a tattered snapshot of his wife Brenda.

Stormin' Norman always let everybody know that he had two families – his own and the men and women under his command.

The 56-year-old career soldier was a 6ft 3ins, 16-stone bear of a man. He graduated from West Point, America's Sandhurst, in 1956, passing out 42nd of 485 officers, and took a degree in missile engineering.

He made his name in Vietnam as a combat adviser to South Vietnamese paratroopers and was twice wounded during active service there.

Schwarzkopf, asked to compare the prospects of a war with Iraq with the war in Vietnam, replied: "To the soldier on the ground it will be exactly the same. We have developed more sophisticated ways of destroying things and the battlefield is more lethal.

"But in to the men in battle it will again simply be a question of life and death. War is a profanity because, let's face it, you've got two opposing sides trying to settle their differences by killing as many of each other as they can. You don't just go out there and say, OK, let's have a nice war today."

He came back from Vietnam as a battalion commander in the 23rd Infantry Division and with a stack of medals including two Purple Hearts. He was posted to command infantry brigades in Alaska and Washington.

It became clear he was being groomed for the top when he was appointed to lead America's elite tank division, the 24th Mechanised Infantry based in Georgia.

He gathered experience in jungle and desert warfare and carved his way up in another kind of warfare – the political infighting waged in the corridors of the Pentagon.

Although he sometimes looked and sounded like a hillbilly backwoodsman, his carefully constructed gung-ho image belied the fact that he held top backroom appointments in Washington as Director of Military Personnel and later as Deputy Chief of Operations and Plans.

But he never lost the ability to see the situation from the viewpoint of the GI. His troops loved him in return.

One paid him the ultimate infantryman's tribute: "He's a very cordial guy, the sort that you wouldn't mind sharing a foxhole with."

OPERATION DESERT STORM

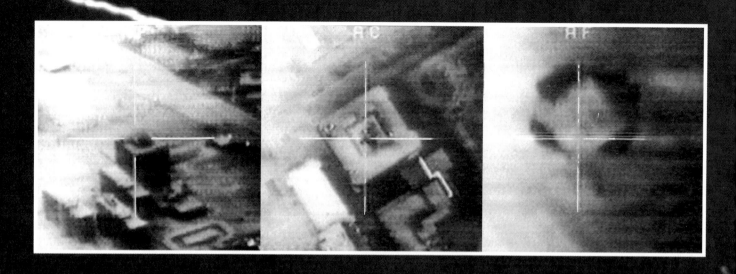

Battle over Baghdad.
Tracer fire lights up the
skyline of the capital.
Inset: An infra-red
sensor of an American
jet outlines the target,
the Iraqi Air Force HQ,
as a laser-guided
missile homes in.

Navy at war: The night sky lights up as a Tomahawk cruise missile is fired at Iraq from the American battleship Wisconsin. Right: The awesome power of the missile is shown as it homes in and then destroys a target during General Dynamics tests in the Californian desert.

IOWA CLASS BATTLESHIP
Displacement: 46,177 tons
Speed: 35 knots
Crew: 1,518
Missiles: 32 Tomahawks

Tomahawk missile launchers

Vulcan Phalanx 20mm six-barrelled gun fires 3,000 rounds a minute

Nine 16 inch guns capable of firing shell weighing 1 ton a distance of 25 miles

TOMAHAWK CRUISE MISSILE
Fly at altitude of 50-300 feet, top speed is 550mph and is accurate to 35 yards over 1,200 miles

Tomahawk launched, path is preprogrammed and follows course plotted onto onboard map

Missile flies low to evade radar, computer checks with terrain contour matching (TERCOM). Final check made just before target is reached.

Faces of war: From a Tornado pilot to the desert masks of Allied troops in the sand, the images of high-tech battle make history in the Nineties

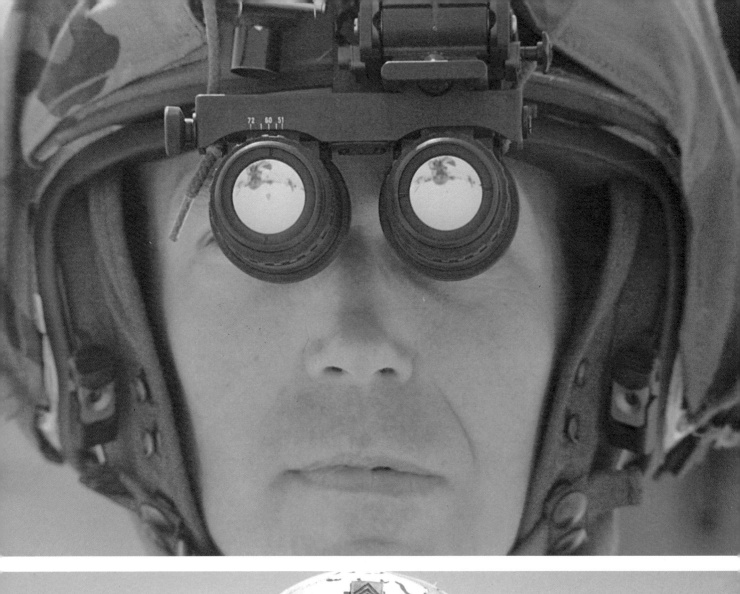

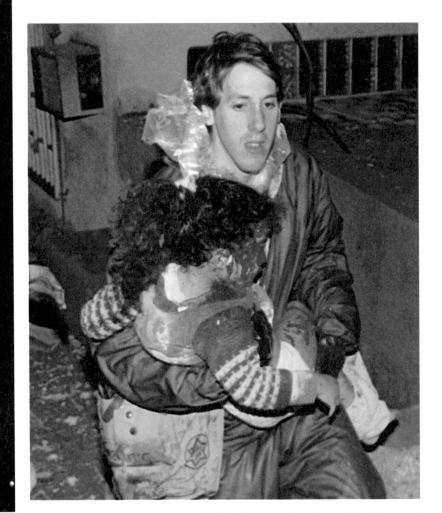

Terror in Tel Aviv: A
Patriot missile blazes
through the sky seeking
out an incoming Iraqi
Scud. This time the
Scud hits its target and a
wounded Israeli child is
rescued from the rubble.
Far right: A Scud shell in
Saudi Arabia

Frontline France:
An impressive array of
French armour rolls
over the Kuwaiti border.
Right: An Iraqi tank
burns after the battle for
Khafji. Centre right: The
black smoke of Kuwait's
blazing Ahmadi oilfield
covers the desert as
U.S. marines penetrate
the Saudi border

Surrender in the sand: Iraqi troops lay by the highway to Kuwait, clutching the surrender note dropped to them by Allied planes at the height of the air bombardment

Liberation day: Kuwaiti troops raise their flag as excited citizens flood the streets of their capital offering victory signs and pictures of the Emir. Iraqi troops however, wave a white flag as a huge column of Allied armour enters the city. But what would the future hold for Kuwait... and its Palestinian citizens?

Escape from Kuwait:
The twisted wreckage of
cars, vans, coaches and
armoured vehicles used
by fleeing Iraqi troops
litters the desert…a
legacy of the invasion
of Kuwait.
Freedom highway. A
town poster of Saddam
lies on the roadside as
an eerie still descends
over Kuwait, hours after
Iraqi troops retreated.

The Desert Prince: Charles leaps onto the sand from a Challenger tank

force to get him out," Cheney said. As he gave his warning air raid sirens wailed in Baghdad and a million citizens, a quarter of the city's population, staged a practice evacuation.

Prince Charles won Whitehall clearance to visit British troops in the desert, but Diana's plan to go with him was vetoed. She would fly to Germany to visit servicemen's families instead. It was thought too dangerous for her to go within range of Saddam's guns only three weeks before the UN deadline for him to quit Kuwait. Government officials also believed that her presence could upset the strict Saudi conventions governing the place of women in society.

The Prince and Princess had argued for two months against diplomatic and security advice in their determination to say a personal Happy Christmas to the men in the front line. There were objections from the Foreign Office and from Downing Street and it was discussed at three Privy Council meetings. The final decision allowing Charles to go was taken by John Major. The Prince would not return from the Gulf until Christmas Eve, which meant that he would miss the christening of Andrew and Fergie's daughter Eugenie at Sandringham Parish Church.

Charles duly arrived in the desert. The first stop was a computer centre which logged all soldiers as they arrived. Charles had to check in like everybody else and when the two lance corporals in charge showed him his computer entry he roared with laughter. For next of kin it listed: "HM Queen Elizabeth II", for blood type: "blue".

Before long Charles was storming through the

dunes on board a Challenger tank, flanked by two others, in a 10-mile drive 100 miles south of the Iraqi lines. The little convoy created its own dust storm as it approached the HQ of the Queen's Royal Irish Hussars, part of the 7th Armoured Brigade. The last time the Prince had been in the Gulf was when he and the Princess visited Kuwait the previous March.

Charles clambered down from the tank and spoke to the men, telling them he was cheered by "their spirit and their great sense of humour". He added: "I have every confidence in the way you perform."

The Hussars' CO, Lieut-Col Arthur Denaro, said: "It was a terrific boost to everyone to see our future King taking time to come and see us."

Charles also met the US troops working closely with the British in the "Anglico" group. Paratrooper Archie Drury, from Clearwater in Florida, said: "It was just great meeting him. We've had the President here but this was the most important person yet. We all love working with the Brits. They keep their feet on the ground and training with them is real sweet."

After being cheered by the entire regiment the Prince board a helicopter to continue his zoom around the desert. He visited a group of sappers with the job of clearing mines. Australian-born Captain Cameron MacNish, 29, handed Charles a boomerang to try. The Prince, who had injured his arm playing polo, hurled it across the sand and said: "That will be good therapy."

Diana was at a bleak British Army base in Hohne, near Hanover in Germany. She told the

Christmas in the Gulf: No snow, no tree. Just sand and an Army Santa for the desert force missing their loved ones at home

750 wives who faced a fraught and lonely Christmas: "You are not forgotten. I just wanted to be with you today to tell you that, especially at Christmas. It's the least I can do. I feel for you." One Army wife said: "We were in the dumps before she came but now we know we are remembered."

Diana being Diana, did not leave out the children. A soldier's son told her he was looking forward to watching Only Fools and Horses on TV over Christmas and the Princess smiled: "That Del Boy is nuts, isn't he?"

The Princess Royal's favourite regiment, the 14/20th King's Hussars of which she was Colonel-in-chief was also bound for the Gulf. The men were leaving without their most prized regimental possession, a magnificent silver chamber pot captured from Napoleon's brother Joseph after the Battle of Victoria in 1816. Tradition had it that the pot was filled with champagne and passed around the Emperor's Chambermaids, as the 14/20th King's Hussars were nicknamed, at regimental dinners. In teetotal Saudi Arabia it would be sadly surplus to requirements.

Tragedy struck the US Navy just before Christmas when a ferry sank killing 20 sailors and injuring 48 off the Israeli port of Haifa. The crewmen, on leave from the aircraft carrier Saratoga, had been ashore for a hard day's Christmas celebrations in the port's bars when they boarded the specially-chartered ferry Tuvia in boisterous spirits for the 20-minute trip back to their ship. High winds and a strong swell made the going difficult. As the 57ft Tuvia plunged through 5ft waves towards the stern of the

Saratoga, the sailors began to move towards the stern to disembark. Two hundred yards from the carrier the Tuvia lurched and started taking water. It sank within seconds, tossing the sailors into the freezing bay.

"All of a sudden tons of water started coming in and the boat started sinking," said one of the 87 survivors. "Everybody started to panic. All I could see was dark. I grabbed this guy's leg and he pulled me out. Thank God I was saved."

Chief petty officer Lance Vickery, 33, said: "If I had been under the water maybe another 30 seconds I wouldn't be talking now."

In Britain men and women in the Territorial Army were urged to sign up for Gulf duty. The Ministry of Defence wrote to doctors and other TA members with medical training asking them to volunteer. Hundreds did but not enough. Eventually buff envelopes marked OHMS dropped on 400 doormats as Defence Secretary Tom King was forced to call up reservists.

It was the biggest call-up since Suez. Defence chiefs needed nurses, theatre technicians and anaesthetists. Some 700 medics with specialist skills had volunteered for active service and Mr King said he was only resorting "with reluctance" to the 1980 Reserve Forces Act to put together a unit of 1,100 to support the 228 full-time medics already preparing for casualties.

The call-up gave reservists the legal guarantee that their jobs would be kept open for them. There was a £210 signing-on fee and plans to top up reservists' salaries by 20 per cent in an effort to make up any shortfall between military pay and civilian medical salaries. For many the top-up would be a drop in the ocean. One £147,000-a-year consultant faced a £92,000 pay cut.

Labour MP Tam Dalyell called on medical reservists to defy the law and refuse to obey their call-up papers. "The purpose of the TA Reserves is the defence of the British Isles, not to form part of an Anglo-American expeditionary force on course for a horrendous war," he said.

At least one man listened. Ex-Private Harry Power, 43, of the Royal Army Medical Corps, said: "I have vowed not to go to the Gulf even if it means being jailed for refusing to serve my country as a reservist. It is not our war. Somewhere along the line someone has to make a stand. If and when war breaks out it is likely to go nuclear at some stage and that is wrong. The ships in the Gulf are armed to the teeth with nuclear missiles. If those things are sent sailing across to Iraq it will be curtains for everybody or, at the very least, it will cause long-lasting and damaging effects worldwide. I have a 13-year-old daughter and I don't want her to be brought up in a world rotten with radioactivity because some Rambo president from America wants to blow Iraq to smithereens." Mr Power's call-up was scrapped.

Families and friends of British soldiers in the Gulf were told they could send Christmas greetings free of charge. In Hampshire a touring pantomime of Aladdin was taken out of its Baghdad setting and the Caliph of Baghdad became the Caliph of Cairo. The Saudis banned Christmas trees.

The Queen, in her Christmas broadcast, spoke of her "deep and over-riding anxiety" over the threat of war. "The servicemen in the Gulf who are spending Christmas at their posts are much in our thoughts," she said. "The invasion of Kuwait was an example on an international scale of an evil which has beset us at different levels in recent years, attempts by ruthless people to impose their will on the peaceable majority."

The Archbishop of Canterbury, Dr Robert Runcie, said in his Christmas message from Canterbury Cathedral that war could be justified as a last resort "if and when all other means of persuasion have failed". The Pope urged national leaders to realise that war would be an adventure with no return.

Chris Buckland of the Daily Express spent Christmas with the troops in the Gulf. He wrote:

"The message of peace on Earth and goodwill to all men echoes untunefully across the moonscaped desert. The unmistakeable aroma of roasting turkey is so strong you can almost touch it. Father Christmas has even put in an appearance, sweltering under his beard and red suit. Presents arrive from all over Britain 100 tons of them, sent by large business corporations, by

old folk digging into their pensions and by children raiding their piggy banks.

"Behind the bravado and manly banter some of these tough lads look close to tears. Choked,' they say quietly. The folks back home are thinking of them. More importantly, they are supporting them. That is a true comfort when you are thousands of miles from your family, stuck in one of Earth's most inhospitable hell holes.

"For security reasons our troops are always said to be somewhere in Saudi Arabia. But they know they are really somewhere between peace and war.

"Flying over the northern Saudi desert for the first time is a humbling experience. A barren landscape that since the beginning of time has only felt the feet of camels and occasional Bedouin tribesmen is now, for hundreds of miles, a heavily-armed camp. New roads criss-cross the dunes. Tanks, missiles, and anti-aircraft defences litter the borderlands for hundreds of miles, there to protect not only Saudi Arabia but the other Gulf states too.

"The airfield where our helicopter was refuelled was like a scene from Apocalypse Now as choppers lined up for a rapid feed. On the road from Dhahran to the Kuwaiti border even Christmas did not stop the never-ending military supply convoys more than 100 vehicles long. The ports have been transformed into vast warehouses of spare parts, tanks, provisions, portaloos foodstuffs and vast water tankers."

Storms swept the British Isles on Christmas Day. They seemed to presage a storm of another kind, brewing in the desert.

 minor storm broke when British military briefing documents went missing in a dangerous security scare. The documents, prepared by Air Chief Marshal Sir Patrick Hine, had been used to brief John Major on British preparedness in the Gulf and were thought to contain the details of British and Allied deployments in the region. Sir Paddy's staff officer, Wing Commander David Farquar, was on his way back to RAF Strike Command at High Wycombe with them when he asked his driver to stop at a car showroom in Acton, West London. They went off to look at the vehicles, leaving the documents in the boot of their own unmarked Vauxhall Carlton.

When they returned the Carlton's boot was open and the documents were gone along with cash, a car TV, a dictaphone and a lap-top computer. The first fear was that Iraqi agents had been active, but it soon became apparent that it seemed to be the work of an opportunist car thief.

Embarrassing, but perhaps not disastrous.

The documents were found dumped in St John's Wood by a doctor who realised their significance and handed them to police. The computer was recovered later. But Wing Commander Farquar was relieved of his post as personal aide to Sir Paddy and the Defence Ministry declined to say what his new duties would be.

New year came and went with the celebrations under a war cloud. People tried not to think what 1991 would bring and plunged into the ritual of parties, champagne and best wishes. The festivities had a strained and frantic air of "Today we dance, for tomorrow we may be at war." Even in Baghdad people poured into the streets, celebrating with their loved ones. In the desert, Allied troops, still on alert, saw the New Year in as best they could with bagpipes, non-alcoholic cocktails, home-grown pantomimes and video shows.

Within hours of the celebrations ending Saddam ordered all 17-year-old males in Iraq to report for military duty.

An intensive, last-ditch round of diplomatic activity began. Luxembourg's foreign minister Jacques Poos announced a peace initiative to Baghdad on behalf of the European Community. He was known to be a cautious man and a cautious politician, in complete contrast to his flamboyant Italian opposite number Gianni de Michelle, from whom he was taking over as Luxembourg embarked on its six-month presidency of the Community. Poos both looked and talked like a sober-suited university professor. He spoke in soft tones, switching effortlessly between French, German and English, and he weighed his words with care. Colleagues said he was predictable with little or no desire to make headline-grabbing gestures. Would this committed European be the answer to the world's prayers?

Britain and America believed that the visit to Baghdad might give Saddam the impression that the Allies were divided. They particularly feared Mr Poos's declaration that an Iraqi withdrawal could be followed by a review of the Israeli-Palestinian question.

Belgium alarmed the Allies further. Prime Minister Wilfried Martens admitted that his forces would run for cover if fighting broke out. His three warships on sanctions patrols "should not become part of an armed conflict", he said. And he turned down a British request for ammunition. MP Teddy Taylor accused Belgium of putting the lives of British soldiers at risk.

World War I folk memories of Gallant Little Belgium went up in smoke.

Mr Poos's mission failed. Then a top French statesman set off for Baghdad on a another breakaway bid for peace. "Unofficial" envoy Michael Vauzelle had more than four hours talks with Saddam, but his errand too was doomed to failure.

The weakening European stand sparked protests from British Tory MPs. Ivan Lawrence of the Commons foreign affairs committee said: "It would be a betrayal of everything the United Nations stands for if its member states did not stand up to its resolutions." Foreign Secretary Douglas Hurd began an intense session of telephone diplomacy with Britain's European partners to stiffen sinews and convince Iraq that the West still meant business.

Iran denounced US "banditry" and warned the Allies that Moslems would "break their legs" if they tried to stay in the Middle East. Teheran leader Ayatollah Ali Khamenei said Arabs in the Gulf states were "disgusted by and despised the foreign presence". He also warned leaders of moderate Gulf states that they would be overthrown if they connived with America. Tension rose when Israel bombed a PLO camp in southern Lebanon, killing 12.

Britain expelled more than 70 Iraqis following a threat by Saddam and his supporters to attack the Allies in their own backyards if the crisis exploded into war. At the top of the expulsion list of mostly students were seven Iraqi envoys and a number of diplomatic staff. They were given 24 hours to get out, the deadline expiring at 9am on January 4, when Britain normally allowed expelled diplomats about a week to arrange their affairs. Douglas Hurd felt he could not wait any longer. "The Iraqis have made a number of public threats," said his spokesman. "It is clearly prudent to take all precautions. The Iraqi threats have once again been linked to the possibility of hostilities. We hope that Iraq complies with the UN Security Council resolutions but time is running out. Threats have been made, and this is a response."

Naiel Abdul-Habbar Hassan, one of the Iraqi embassy staff officials thrown out, told journalists as he left Heathrow: "If Iraq is going to be a target, then all the Western Allies will be targets. Arabs in Britain will launch something against many targets if Iraq is attacked."

In Baghdad, an Iraqi Government spokesman said: "Our country denounces this unjustified step and considers it part of a series of measures reflecting aggression and hated colonial mentality. We reserve the right to retaliate."

A security net was thrown around Saudi

Waiting for war. Desert Rats sit round a camp fire in the sand as the cold chill of war and winter descends

Arabia's oilfields, the world's biggest, in case of suicide attacks by terrorists. Hundreds of extra troops and anti-aircraft batteries were moved to guard the oil wells. Iraq was already reported to have mined wells in Kuwait. The SAS was put on standby to defend Britain's North Sea oil rigs.

As 13 more warships carrying 7,500 Marines set sail from the Philippines for the Gulf, President Bush held his first New Year briefing with his top military advisers. He claimed, at least publicly, that he did not know what he would do if Saddam failed to quit Kuwait on January 15.

"I suppose if I knew exactly I wouldn't advertise it because there are a lot of lives at stake. All options are open," he said in a Washington TV interview.

Hours later Jordan's King Hussein flew into London for talks with John Major. British women and children were urged to get out of Jordan and Yemen before the UN deadline.

The world waited for Saddam to respond to another overture by President Bush for peace in the Gulf. He had given the Iraqi leader until January 5 to reply to an offer to send Secretary of State Baker to Geneva to meet his Iraqi opposite number Tariq Aziz. Iraq was studying the proposals.

President Bush, in a radio broadcast to the American people, said his sincere hope was that 1991 would be a year of peace. But he stressed: "We are ready to use force to defend a new order emerging among the nations of the world, a world of sovereign nations living in peace."

He said Saddam posed a strategic threat to Egypt, Saudi Arabia, Israel, Turkey and Syria. "Each day that passes brings Saddam further on the path to developing biological and nuclear weapons and the missiles to deliver them," the President again said. He rejected arguments that Allied forces should wait longer to allow economic sanctions more time to work, warning that Iraqi forces were digging in deep in Kuwait. "We risk paying a higher price in the most precious currency of all, human life, if we give Saddam more time to prepare for war," he said.

Intelligence reports were indeed painting a gloomy picture. Saddam's war machine was building up for conflict. Another 20,000 soldiers, plus artillery, poured into Kuwait. Iraq also laid more mines in the Gulf.

Iraq finally agreed to meet the Americans for talks in Geneva on Wednesday January 9. The Allies welcomed Baghdad's decision, but Tariq Aziz imposed a condition on any peace package the discussion of the Israeli-Palestinian issue. Another Iraqi official warned the talks would last "only five minutes" unless America softened.

Tariq Aziz burst out laughing before an audience of millions of American TV viewers when asked if Baghdad would offer to withdraw from Kuwait to avoid a bloodbath. "Never, never!" he said. "Kuwait is part of Iraq now. We will not start a war but if there is one it will be long and bloody."

President Bush warned Saddam that he had a week to choose between peace or battle. "The danger in all this should be clear to all," he said. "The price of peace now on Saddam's terms will be paid many times over in greater sacrifice, in suffering. Saddam's power will only grow, along with his appetite for more conquest. The next conflict will find him stronger still, perhaps in possession of nuclear weapons."

The US-Iraqi talks were doomed from the

start. They went to Geneva and could not even agree which shape table to sit round. The Hotel Intercontinental had to fax Baghdad and Washington for guidance. Then the teams haggled over the venue of their historic talks, eventually settling for a ground floor conference room with a baize table.

When the two nine-man teams came face to face, the tension was clear from the start. Photographers allowed in for pre-talks pictures said Baker and Aziz agreed to pose shaking hands, and did, but the harmony immediately evaporated. They sat and stared at each other. For a long period there was no chit-chat, no conversation. Only a few opening questions broke the cold silence.

Both sides were a stern bunch drawn from the top tables of their foreign affairs teams. Aziz, an urbane diplomat with fluent English, was flanked by his interpreter and Iraq's ambassador to the UN in Geneva, Barzan al-Tikriti Saddam's powerful half-brother. He was thought to be keeping a close watch on Aziz, ready to give the nod to any Iraqi bid to forge a deal. He had played peacemaker before, bringing Iran and Iraq together for talks in 1988.

Opposite was Secretary of State Baker, backed by his top Middle East specialist John Kelly and one of President Bush's chief military advisers, Lieutenant General Howard Graves.

Most observers expected the talks to break up within two or three hours. Some predicted that the Iraqis would storm out when Mr Baker launched into an hour-long speech on the power of the multinational force ranged against Saddam. Yet Baker and Aziz held not one, not two, but three rounds of talks. They lasted seven hours. Baker postponed his evening flight to Turkey to try to go that extra mile for peace pledged more than once by his boss, President Bush. The teams kept silent between sessions, refraining from the rhetoric from both Washington and Baghdad which had marked the five-month countdown to conflict. Even a half-hearted peace protest outside the hotel fizzled out.

Inevitably, the talks collapsed. Aziz even refused to carry a letter back to Baghdad. Then came the rhetoric. Saddam warned that American troops "would swim in their own blood". Aziz again threatened Israel. President Bush described the Iraqi display at the lakeside summit as a "total stiff-arm, a total rebuff".

French President Francois Mitterrand said war with Iraq was "critically certain." King Hussein of Jordan pleaded: "We must not resign ourselves totally to the inevitability of war. There are still a few days to go." A Saudi government spokesman said: "We must prepare ourselves for bloodshed. It is a terrible tragedy."

Only a hastily announced last-minute mission by UN Secretary Peres de Cuellar could stop a bloodbath.

A few days before Saddam's invasion of

BAKER: ONE LAST MILE FOR PEACE FROM THE MAN CLOSEST T(

James Baker was the tough-talking Texan behind America's uncompromising foreign policy stance in the Gulf.

The sixty-year-old lawyer became US Secretary of State in his friend George Bush's administration in 1989, and his close relationship with the President meant everybody knew that when Baker spoke Bush's lips moved.

Bush and Baker first met more than thirty years ago, and have been inseparable, both in politics and on the tennis court ever since.

Both were sons of Texas, Bush by adoption and Baker by birth. Baker was born into one of Houston's most illustrious families which had grown rich in the practice of the law. It was pre-ordained that Baker would become an attorney.

But James Addison Baker the Third was still doused with cold water by his father if he lay in bed after 7 am.

His father's puritanical upbringing paid off, and the young Baker soon adopted his lifetime habit of hard work and clean living. He became a successful lawyer in Houston after graduating from Princeton and Austin University.

In his degree treatise Baker chose to contrast two British politicians – both Labour. He masterly summed up the careers of Aneurin Bevan and the postwar Foreign Secretary Ernest Bevin.

"Bevin was interested in practicalities, not in theories," he wrote. Baker adopted the same philosophy, saying later "I am not a man of vision – I don't pretend to be one."

He was brought up as a Democrat but converted to Republicanism when his first wife Mary became involved in their friend George Bush's campaign for a seat in Congress.

The death of Mary, from cancer at the age of 38, was a central tragedy in Baker's life. Congressman Bush came to the rescue persuading him to help him in his re-election campaign.

The therapy worked, and Baker later married one of Mary's friends. By that time the politics bug had bitten deeply, and he rose rapidly through the Republican party to become Under-Secretary of Commerce in President Ford's Cabinet.

He masterminded Ford's re-election campaign, bringing him to within a whisker of beating Jimmy Carter.

He went on to run the Bush campaign against Reagan for the nomination in 1980 – Bush lost but Baker's adroit manipulation got him the Vice-Presidency and put him in the White House when Reagan stepped down.

Baker's three passions, according to friends, were sleeping, working and hunting – especially for Texas wild turkeys.

One of his fellow hunters said: "Jim never liked to take too many chances – he used to hire a guy to lay out some corn for the turkeys and then shot them while they ate."

His approach to foreign policy proved to be much the same.

Kuwait, de Cuellar had been thumbing through brochures looking for a farm to buy in his home country of Peru, telling colleagues he was ready to retire now the world was a safer place. His wife Marcela and his doctors had been pestering him to stand down, fearing for his health after heart surgery. Under his calm stewardship the UN had won back world respect. The Cold War was over, the blue berets of the peace-keeping forces had won a Nobel prize and much of the credit reflected on the 70-year-old, grey-haired career diplomat. Now, instead of spending his twilight years in peace and tranquility, he was thrust back on to the dangerous world stage.

Any hopes that the UN peacemaker would succeed with his five-point plan centred on a UN peacekeeping force for Kuwait and vague promises of a Middle East peace conference were dashed on the day his plane touched down in Baghdad. Saddam announced to the world that he expected war.

He told 150 cheering delegates during a surprise appearance at an Islamic conference that his nation would win. In a 40-minute speech he said he would use chemical weapons in a Holy War between the infidels and the believers "the true and the untrue." Saddam derided the Allied forces ranged against him. "They may try playing acrobatics as in the Rambo movies, but they will be devoured by wolves," he said.

Arab diplomats suggested, perhaps wistfully, that Saddam was deliberately raising the temperature before making a grand gesture just ahead of the UN deadline. Their hopes were dashed when his information minister, Latif Nassif al-Jassem, dismissed even a partial withdrawal from Kuwait.

De Cuellar's mission failed. So too did last-ditch attempts by France and Germany.

 t the Sheraton Hotel in the Saudi Arabian resort of Taif, 70 miles from the Red Sea, the Emir of Kuwait handed John Major a 40-page album decorated in gold.

This was no collection of souvenir happy snaps. It was a dossier of atrocities allegedly committed by Iraqis in Kuwait. There were photographs of butchered Kuwaitis in a portfolio of murder, rape and torture. There were stories of children being shot in front of their parents. Of men having their fingernails ripped out, and worse.

The Prime Minister was horrified. He pledged that the Emir's country would be freed from tyranny. Kuwait had been reduced to a prison camp in which atrocities were being committed daily, he said. He vowed that Britain was ready to go to war. A transformation was taking place under the desert sun. John Major was travelling down the perilous road from Prime Minister to war leader. As his Puma helicopter skimmed low over the sand where herds of camels wandered nonchalantly among the world's most

THE PRESIDENT OF AMERICA... IN POLITICS AND ON THE TENNIS COURT

The door to war cannot be bolted. To the dismay of Moslems and Christians alike, UN Secretary General Perez de Cuellar failed to tie the rope of peace

sophisticated weaponry, he realised the enormity of the mission facing them. He knew that in less than a week he could be asked to send the Desert Rats, the RAF and the Royal Navy into a bloody war which would stamp its mark on history however it turned out.

Barely 60 miles from the Iraqi enemy in occupied Kuwait and just 41 days into his Premiership, he was adamant that he would not shrink from taking that decision because of the principle that made it a right thing to do. Gone was his familiar pin-striped suit as he stepped out on the front line. There was no gung-ho flak jacket, but a casual sand-coloured open neck shirt, fawn trousers and sensible Clarkes shoes.

The reception was less than ecstatic. "I would rather get Kate Adie's autograph," said one soldier of the 14th-20th Kings's Hussars, daring to approach the BBC's formidable reporter. Signaller Mark Porter, 27, of the Royal Signals, said: "Major has only just come into power and there is no comparison with Mrs Thatcher. She got us through the Falklands, didn't she?"

Mrs Thatcher was widely known to be good at troop visits. But as Mr Major swept through the sand dunes in a Challenger tank the new recruit at Number 10 started to win his admirers. He was praised when he said, simply: "I wanted to come and see for myself what is happening here. There is a tremendous amount of pride and affection, if I may say so, in how you are preparing for what may lie ahead. Unless Saddam Hussein gets out of Kuwait and gets back into Iraq we will invite you to remove him. Whatever needs to be done could not be in better hands."

He pledged to take home any complaints from the troops to be investigated by Defence Secretary Tom King to make life in the desert a little more comfortable for The Rats. The biggest gripe in a land without liquor and nightlife was a lack of recreational facilities and British newspapers. There was also some jealousy from the troops about the American love boats. They had heard of British strippers hired to entertain the GIs on the floating hotels.

Mr Major could not promise cruises and exotic dancers. He did report that England had at last drawn a Test Match in Australia and predicted that Graham Gooch's men would now go on to square the Ashes series. Sadly, he was wrong.

Only a British Prime Minister could be endearingly capable of boosting morale with cricket scores on the eve of a holocaust. For now, the deadline was truly upon us.

T he seconds ticked down on millions of clocks watched by millions of eyes. Then it was here … midnight on January 15, New York time, the irrevocable expiry of the UN deadline.

It was 8am in Iraq. "Welcome to the Holy War," read the headline in the newspaper.

People on the streets of Baghdad were determined to show that they were not afraid as the deadline struck. Mothers chanted for the TV cameras then, after a couple of minutes, scooped their children under their arms and melted away like the morning mist. It was a thick, clammy morning and, raising their eyes to the heavens, some in the crowd comforted one another by agreeing that not even the Americans would fly in such weather. Within an hour most streets were deserted and shops empty. Normally bustling bazaars had their shutters down. Street cafes had none of the well-dressed young men who for weeks had been sipping their thick black Arab coffee and talking of nothing else but when the Americans would back down. Taxi drivers, sensing it might be their last day of business for some time, charged twelve times their usual fares. Many, convinced that the Saudis would never let the infidels desecrate Moslem shrines with their missiles, joined a procession of cars snaking south to the holy Iraqi cities of Nejef and Kerbala. The Government, running out of gas masks, issued charcoal for citizens to make their own crude filters. Suddenly the most popular places in Baghdad were those with cavernous steel-plated air raid shelters, like the Al Rasheed hotel where the dwindling band of foreign journalists waited.

There was another eerie silence on the streets of Jerusalem and Tel Aviv. Behind the shutters people waited nervously for the often-threatened Iraqi aerial onslaught which would drag them into war. Schools were closed and one in five hospital patients were sent home to free beds for war casualties. In Jerusalem, ultra-orthodox Jews danced and prayed at the Wailing Wall, revered as the last remnant of the ancient Jewish temple. Hundreds of thousands of Palestinians in Gaza and at the West Bank were kept in their homes by a curfew enforced by thousands of Israeli troops. The only sign of life was in Tel Aviv restaurants where jean-clad teenagers, many with automatic rifles slung over their shoulders, held discos. They called them End of the World Parties.

In Riyadh, Saudi Arabia, life seemed to go on as normal. Ostentatious American cars plied between the homes of rich Saudis and their ultra-modern government offices down King Fahd Street. Shops and offices were full of people going about their business.

Jordan feared that it would become embroiled in war. King Hussein went on television to declare that his armed force of 100,000 men would "prevent anyone, whosoever, from crossing our land and skies in any direction". Army reservists were called up.

In Washington anti-terrorist measures were in operation at the Pentagon, around Congress, the White House, the FBI and CIA headquarters and other key government buildings. Several thousand anti-war demonstrators marched, bedraggled in the rain, as they continued a vigil being maintained in cities and towns across the US. It was a tense day of prayer and hope against hope that Saddam would back down.

Downing Street announced that 28 more Iraqis were to be kicked out because of threats to national security. France put its 12,000 troops under American command. Saddam appointed himself Field Marshal and took personal control of his army.

In Britain's pre-dawn darkness, tanks and armoured cars stood guard at airports in the biggest security alert since World War II. Armed soldiers patrolled Heathrow and passengers' luggage was scrupulously checked.

The world held its breath. Saddam held his ground.

Our thoughts are with you. John Major brings hope and strength to the Desert Rats in Saudi

CHAPTER 7

THE GULF WAR

'White flashes are everywhere! Bullets are being fired. The sky is lit up. It looks like a million fireflies!'

TV reporter John Holliman

President George Bush sat hunched over his desk in the Oval Office staring at the red telephone. He had already used the same phone to talk to his commanders in Saudi Arabia. His final words had been: "May God go with you." Now timing was everything.

The White House staff were getting ready to go home. They were speculating, like everyone else, about a land war. No one really knew. The President had only confided in a handful of close confidantes, who now sat with their Commander in Chief. Each was lost in his own thoughts.

For days President Bush had agonised over how long to wait before unleashing the most awesome firepower the world had ever witnessed. He had listened to everyone's advice and prayed that Saddam would see sense and pull out of Kuwait. He told his war cabinet that the final decision for war would be his and his alone.

The red telephone rang. The President reached for it and cradled the receiver close to his ear. He nodded once, saying only: "Thank you."

Taking off his gold-rimmed spectacles, he rubbed his eyes and told his aides: "Gentlemen, it has begun."

"White flashes are everywhere! Bullets are being fired into the air! The whole sky is lit up with gunfire! It looks like a million fireflies!"

The words of American TV reporter John Holliman, crackling through the airways as he hung out of his Baghdad hotel window, told the world that war had begun.

It was 2.44am, January 17, 1991, in Baghdad. Waves of American, British and Saudi jets and missiles were blasting key military and communications sites throughout Iraq. Bat-winged Stealth bombers joined F1-11s and giant B52s to drop 18,000 tons of explosives in five hours, equivalent to a Hiroshima atom bomb and a half, and double the destruction that fell on the German city of Dresden.

At the same time RAF Tornado GR1 bombers from Saudi Arabia and Bahrain and American

F15E fighter bombers, aided by 150 Saudi fighters, took off to hit other airbases and radar installations around Basra, Iraq's second city.

Less than 20 hours after the expiry of the UN deadline a pyrotechnic display of anti-aircraft tracer fire and bomb bursts lit up the moonless sky over Baghdad. Streets, flats and office blocks were still brilliantly lit because Saddam had neglected to order a black-out.

Sophisticated cruise missiles, Tomahawks with a range of 1,500 miles, were launched from the giant US battleships Wisconsin and Missouri in the Gulf, to land with precision on Saddam's airfields and his command and control centres. The Tomahawks, their warheads packed with conventional high-explosive, had state-of-the-art guidance technology which made them accurate to within inches. The ship-to-shore missiles flew to near speed-of-sound at heights of 50ft to 350ft, hugging the contours of the land and ducking Iraqi radar.

Saddam's ostentatious Baghdad palace received a direct hit. So did the Iraqi parliament building. Scud missile sites ranged against Israel were also bombed along with nuclear and chemical weapons centres.

Operation Desert Storm was under way. The world watched it live on TV. The sound of muffled explosions mingled with the spitting cracks of anti-aircraft fire. Reporter Holliman dangled his microphone out of the window to catch the sounds of battle. He described the mayhem outside as "fireworks on the Fourth of July" and shouted: "The sirens are going off, it's happening! Just listen!"

The thuds and crashes could be heard along with the wailing sirens. Never had history been made so vividly. The TV networks were recording every second of the attack. At one point Holliman dramatically lost his line out of Baghdad, sparking fears that the Al-Rasheed hotel, less than a mile from Saddam's palace, had been hit.

But he was reconnected minutes later and as the noise of automatic gunfire filled the airway, Holliman shouted again: "The attack seems to be centred on the airport. Tonight every bomb we have seen seems to have hit something. They have hit the refinery, the communications centre...the guided bomb missiles system seems to be proving it is deadly accurate. The whole building is shaking. The bombs are landing all around us but the town is still lit up. It's incredible! Baghdad is still a blaze of lights despite the bombing. In the sky we can see tracer rounds aimed at the aircraft. Only now are they beginning to impose a blackout. There's a huge column of smoke hanging over Baghdad."

At one stage Holliman and the two other CNN

'The liberation of Kuwait has begun. We will not fail. Our forces will not fight with one hand tied behind their backs.'

George Bush

Desert Storm. May God be with you."

A few hours later President Bush spoke solemnly to the world from his office in the White House. In a moving 12-minute address he pledged that the Allies were going to "chart the future of the world for a hundred years." He vowed: "The liberation of Kuwait has begun. We will not fail."

The emirate had been "crushed, then brutalised" and military action had been taken only after months of "constant and virtually endless" diplomatic activity, the President said.

"Our forces will not be asked to fight with one hand tied behind their backs," he pledged, calming military memories of the stop-go shambles of Vietnam. "We are determined to knock out Saddam Hussein's nuclear bomb potential. We will also destroy his chemical weapons facilities. Much of his tanks and artillery will be destroyed. This is an historic moment. We have the opportunity to forge a new world order.

"I am hopeful that this fighting will not go on for long and casualties will be held to an absolute minimum. Saddam's forces will leave Kuwait, the legitimate government will be restored and the country will once again be free and then when peace is restored it is our hope that Iraq will live as a peaceful and co-operative member of the family of nations.

"Some ask: Why not wait? The answer is clear. The world could wait no longer. Sanctions showed no sign of having accomplished their objectives. Sanctions were tried for over five months, but we have concluded that they would not force Saddam from Kuwait.

"While we waited, Saddam pillaged and plundered a tiny nation. He subjected the people of Kuwait to untold atrocities. While the world waited, Saddam sought to add to his chemical weapons an infinitely more dangerous weapon, a nuclear one. And while the world waited, Saddam dug in."

The President said the decision to send "our sons and daughters" to war was not made easily. But he was persuaded because: "The terrible crimes and tortures committed by Saddam's

correspondents with him, Bernie Shaw and Peter Arnett, crawled under their beds. Shaw shouted: "It feels like we're in the centre of hell!"

Baghdad radio ignored the Allied attacks at first and broadcast quotations from the Moslem holy book, the Koran. Later the voice of Saddam came on the air announcing: "The mother of battles has begun! Satan Bush has committed his crime!"

There was no sign of Iraqi fighter planes in the sky. Pentagon chiefs were baffled as to why Saddam had not hit back, hard. There were two possible explanations; either the Allied strike had eliminated his defensive capability or he was saving his war machine to fight another day.

Meanwhile General Schwarzkopf announced to the 660,000 Allied troops in the desert: "You must be the thunder and lightning of Operation

POWER OF THE PROWLER: NO BOMBS...JUST RADIO WAVES AND ELECTRONS

One of the most deadly weapons in the Gulf fired only streams of radio waves and electrons.

It was the American EA-6B Prowler aircraft, whose mission was to jam Iraq's ground-based early warning radars and anti-aircraft missile fire control systems.

There were at least 20 Prowlers in the Gulf operating from the US Navy's carrier fleet. The aircraft are fitted with the latest avionic systems and carry five pods each containing two jamming transmitters. The jammers are powered by turbine blades driven by the plane's slipstream, which makes hardware

failure much less likely. Each pod can generate seven different frequencies and jam two of them simultaneously, either automatically or on command.

Wingtip sensors on the Prowler pick up incoming radar waves and feed them into a central computer. A lone Prowler accompanying a bombing raid can blind all the radars at the target. One of the the intelligence titbits the Soviets handed over to the Pentagon was the radar frequency of Iraq's Soviet-made anti-aircraft missiles. Once Iraq's radar system was jammed, SAS teams pinpointed targets with laser pistols.

henchmen against the innocent people of Kuwait are an affront to mankind and a challenge to the freedom of all."

Prime Minister Major had been told personally over a telephone hotline by President Bush the precise time that war would break out. Mr Major stayed awake all night with top officials, watching the TV bulletins and following developments. Contact was kept with the White House amid hopes that the initial raids on Baghdad's communciation and military targets would lead to an early surrender. The full details of the attack came into Downing Street from Britain's war command centre at High Wycombe.

At 7am, the Prime Minister emerged from Downing Street to praise the skill and bravery of British Tornado pilots and navigators. President Bush rang to thank him for Britain's unstinting contribution to the Gulf effort. The Pentagon, announcing that 80 per cent of Allied planes had hit their designated targets, said: "The Tornados were tops. You couldn't ask for more from allies fighting by your side."

The Labour Party was quick to throw its weight behind the war and appealed for a swift end to the conflict. Despite the bitter divisions within his party leader Neil Kinnock said: "Now that war has started, everyone will hope it will be as short as possible with the minimum of casualties."

In the US the Chairman of the Joint Chiefs of Staff, General Colin Powell, praised the air crews who had taken part in the raids. And he warned Saddam that he had not begun to see "all the tools in the toolbox". But both Downing Street and the White House stressed that the Allies should not get complacent. Iraq still had a huge arsenal of weapons and 2,600 tanks in Kuwait. The first casualties on the Allied side were seven jets, although Iraq claimed to have shot down 55. The Allies reported the loss of three US aircraft a 5E Strike Eagle, an F/A-18 Hornet fighter bomber and an A-6 Intruder bomber.

Britain lost two Tornado GR1 ground attack planes, each with two crew. The Kuwaiti government-in-exile announced that one of its Skyhawks had been lost. One of Italy's 10 Tornados failed to return.

Apart from these, the only confirmed Western casualties were three US soldiers hurt in a missile attack on a shut-down, Japanese-owned oil refinery near the town of Khafji in Eastern Saudi Arabia. It was the only sign of Iraqi aggression in the first 24 hours and was later to be the scene of a dramatic street battle.

Most surprising to the Allied commanders was the lack of Iraqi air resistance. Although returning crews reported heavy anti-aircraft artillery and missiles there was still scarcely a sign of the 700-plane Iraqi air force with its highly-rated MiG 29s.

As 50 Iraqi tanks surrendered to Egypt's 4th

Smoke rises from downtown Baghdad after the first Allied blitz.

'I clawed for my little sisters with my bare hands in the rubble...I just wanted them to live.'

Shantov Davidy

Armoured Division, and a steady trickle of deserters crossed the Turkish and Saudi frontiers, six MiGS were reported downed and Captain Stephen Tate, flying a US F-15 fighter, claimed the war's first dogfight victory by shooting down an Iraqi Mirage F-1 while escorting bombers over Baghdad.

The RAF's £18 million Tornados had flown from their bases accompanied by Victor and VC10 refuelling tankers to extend their range. Tornado pilots returning safely to their bases told of how the flying petrol tanks were a welcome sight in the clouds after their bombing runs. One British pilot described the skies filled with flak and anti-aircraft fire as he flew in to bomb an Iraqi airfield. "It was the scariest thing I have ever done," said Flt Lt Ian Long, 25, of 31 Squadron. "It was unbelievable. There was a lot of flak out to our right. As we approached the airfield boundary we saw the weapons go off just to our left hand side. We ran like hell. You are frightened of failure, you are frightened of dying. You are flying as low as you dare and high enough to get the weapons off. You push it as low as you can over the target and get away as fast as you can."

The celebratory clenched fists from cockpits needed no interpretation as pilots arrived back on desert airstrips from sorties flown at 600mph and less than 100ft up. Pilots and navigators climbed down cockpit steps to cheers. "It ran on rails," said one pilot, relief written into his face. "Now we are going to have to wait and see what we have achieved."

Another told back-slapping colleagues: "It was frightening, but I've got to go and do it all over again. It was all over the place up there. We were flying with night goggles so you couldn't see for miles. You could see flashes from the ground."

He described the return journey after dropping his payload of bombs on military and communication installations in Iraq and Kuwait. "When we joined the tankers we were almost out of fuel," he said. "It was nice to see them. They were a friendly sight. They were in cloud and it was great to link up."

The pilots' wives in Britain and Germany had been glued to televisions and radios, some clinging to each other for support. Secretary Debbie Carrington, 27, moved from Norwich to a hotel near her fiance Bill Porter's former UK airbase in Coltishall so she could get immediate information about him.

"When I woke up this morning and heard it was war I just couldn't believe it," she said. "I know he has a job to do. When you fall in love with a serviceman that is something you just have to put up with."

Coltishall village was uneasily quiet as conflicting reports continued over the involvement of the RAF base's 12-strong Jaguar squadron in the Gulf. Village deputy post master Harvey Meadows said: "You wouldn't think there was anything going on the Gulf. Nobody is talking about it."

he light of dawn broke over Baghdad on the morning after the first raids. The precision of the bombing was such that the city centre seemed relatively unscathed. A trickle of traffic and a few bemused Iraqis emerged on to the streets, while CNN reported that radio transmission masts and the telephone exchange seemed undamaged.

The Allies congratulated themselves on their initial success while generals and politicians warned of complacency. John Major told a packed House of Commons: "We should be under no illusion whatsoever about the scale and potential might of the Iraqi forces. While I am confident of success, I am not confident about the speed of that success."

Waves of bombers and Tomahawk cruise missiles carried on pounding Saddam's men and military installations throughout the day. President Bush called on the Iraqi leader to save lives and surrender now. He praised the pilots and agreed with Mr Major that there should be no "pause for peace" until Iraq pulled out ot Kuwait.

Relieved stock markets around the world soared in response to the apparent swift success of the Allied attack. Petrol companies abandoned a proposed 10p a gallon increase and actually planned a cut in the cost of four-star and unleaded at the pumps.

Thousands of refugees fleeing the bombardment headed into Jordan. TV reporters kept up their 24-hour broadcasts. BBC Television's John Simpson told how he watched as a cruise missile glided past his Baghdad hotel window in silence, homing in on its target.

While Western newspapers were reporting that three top military advisers to Saddam had been executed because of their poor response to the Allied attack, Iraqi TV showed pictures of their leader walking through the streets of Baghdad. He was pictured being hugged and congratulated by excited soldiers in the miles of corridors linking him to his underground headquarters. The world also saw Field Marshall Saddam, as he had promoted himself, kneeling in prayer in a bunker.

Baghdad radio interrupted programmes of martial music to broadcast a letter from Saddam to President Bush, diplomatically addressed to: "The Enemy of God and Colleague of the Devil."

The letter warned that American blood would

flow. Saddam vowed that war would topple Mr Bush, Saudi Arabia's King Fahd and the British monarchy. It would also liberate Palestine and conquer Israel. The Allies prepared more prison camps in Saudi Arabia.

Protests against the war started to be heard. In Washington mounted police charged banner-waving demonstrators outside the White House. Fourteen people were arrested when chanting activists started fighting with Bush supporters. But a Washington Post-ABC TV news poll showed that 76 per cent of Americans backed President Bush's action.

Anti-war protestors marched by torchlight in Germany. In Australia others wept at a midday sit-in. In Paris security cordons surrounded the British embassy after fighting broke out. In Jordan, King Hussein's government condemned the war. The country's large Palestinian population vowed vengeance on the West.

In Britain, leaders of all parties were united. Neil Kinnock said Saddam could prevent further "death and destruction" by laying down his arms and complying with international law. He supported Mr Major in believing that "the conflict was not wanted by those allied against Iraq and was therefore regretted."

He added: "For the sake of our forces and their families, and for the sake of innocent civilians in Kuwait and Iraq, people everywhere will hope that success in fulfilling the purposes of the UN is achieved as speedily as possible."

Edward Heath added: "Now that war had sadly come we must give all our support to our forces." Mrs Thatcher warned: "Dictators do not surrender, they have to be well and truly defeated."

ADDAM made good his threats against Israel and unleashed his Scud missiles. In the dark hours before dawn on Friday morning, January 18, eight Soviet-designed Scud-B missiles, stretched by Iraqi engineers to extend their range, exploded in Israel as air raid sirens sounded and families in gas masks rushed into sealed rooms and shelters, fearing a chemical attack. Another Scud dropped on Dhahran in Saudi Arabia.

Israel was lucky. There was no huge death toll. Three of the Scuds landed harmlessly in uninhabited countryside. Five got through to the packed cities of Tel Aviv and Haifa, injuring 12.

It was the development everyone had feared. Israel, in all its 42-year history, had never failed to respond to any attack on its territory. Yet no Arab leader in the coalition could escape intense criticism or even a national uprising if he was

Image of war: Two Israeli soldiers stand in the ruins of Tel Aviv after a Scud missile attack.

seen to be supporting Jerusalem. With Egypt, Syria, Oman, Bahrain, Turkey, Saudi Arabia, the United Arab Emirates and Morocco all pledging troops, bases and resources to back the anti-Saddam coalition, Israeli retaliation could easily force a large part of the Islamic contingent to change sides. Every ounce of diplomatic leverage was needed.

In Israel there had been fatalities. Four people suffocated inside their gas masks three Israeli women and a three-year-old Arab girl. Two of the women and the little girl died because they had not removed a plastic seal on their masks. One old woman suffered respiratory and heart problems wearing her protective breathing gear.

In one Tel Aviv street two sleeping girls had a lucky escape when one of the missiles exploded 20 yards away. Eight-year-old Odid Davidy and her six-year-old sister Hadvid were in bed when rubble smashed into their room, blasting a 10ft hole in the wall.

Their brother Shantov, a 19-year-old soldier, said: "I clawed for them with my bare hands. I wanted them to live and I was frightened there would be gas."

Shantov, still in shock, stood in the hall of the shattered home as he recalled the attack. "I was listening to a Beatles record when there was this huge explosion," he said. "I was thrown to the ground and all I could hear was the shattering of glass and the crashing of walls.

"Then there was screaming, sobbing and moaning. I was shaken but I first helped my grandmother who lives with us. We put on gas masks and I went and got my sisters who were bleeding and hurt. Then we all went to the school nearby with the injured. The Mayor arrived and thankfully told us there was no gas, no one had been killed and God would help us. But my sisters are just little girls and I am very angry they should be hurt like this while they sleep."

Daily Express reporter Alun Rees was in Tel Aviv as the Scuds fell. He said: "Fear, gas masks and the man behind the World Cup anthem combined to make the night of the first rocket strike a surreal experience I will never forget.

"Outside the Tel Aviv Hilton I watched the flame trail of a Scud missile before reaching for my gas mask and safety. I felt the massive thud as the missile struck the suburbs some miles away. From that point, the night took on an air of unreality as I headed with hundreds of others for the Hilton's specially-prepared shelter.

"Every gap over every door and window had been sealed with masking tape and polythene, and I looked with disbelief down the long corridor where we sat. It was like some ghastly tube train, stuck in a tunnel. All the passengers

were wearing gas masks. You could almost reach out and grasp the fear.

"In this unlikely setting I was to meet one of my heroes, conductor Zubin Mehta, who brought together Pavarotti, Domingo and Carreras for the unforgettable World Cup concert in Rome. Our conversation took place through frog-eyed masks, the rasp of breath obscuring some of our words.

"Hello, Maestro, I said. I know it's a strange place to say this, but I thought your concert in Rome was wonderful. I wish we were there now." He replied, 'So do I. Have you English lost another plane today?'

"I think so, I replied. None shall sleep tonight." He nodded, "Nessun dorma."

As President Bush threw a protective shield of Patriot missile batteries and expert operators around Israel, Allied bombers were ordered to seek out and destroy Saddam's mobile Scud missile launchers.

Israeli public opinion was clamouring for a strike against Iraq.

In a series of urgent telephone calls the White House urged the Israeli Cabinet, which was meeting in almost permanent session, to show restraint.

Six mobile Scud launch sites found in Iraq were destroyed hours later. "We shall attack these sites relentlessly," vowed General Schwarzkopf. But he admitted that finding them was like looking for a needle in a haystack.

Thirty six of Saddam's permanent missile sites were believed to have been destroyed. Pentagon officials said Iraq had about another 30 mobile launchers left. Still there was the fear that these would have chemical warheads.

Two families of British Tornado pilots were saying special prayers. Flt Lt John Peters, 28, and his navigator Adrian Nichol, 27, were missing. In North Shields Adrian's father John, 68, said: "All we can do is pray,"

In Baghdad, BBC foreign affairs editor John Simpson sent another despatch on his satellite telephone. Speaking to David Dimbleby live on screen in London he said: "We know that there have been civilian casualties. I've not heard of anybody actually dying but I've heard of people being injured. There's shrapnel around and that can hit people. It's inevitable there must be deaths."

He had seen another Tomahawk missile flying down the street past his hotel window after filming one the night before. "It passed by just a few minutes ago about 100 feet above the ground. I have no idea what it hit," he said. "They

obviously go down the same routes quite a lot." Moments later his guard returned and Simpson's line went dead.

The precision of the Allied bombing was displayed to the world by American commanders. The West's computers had plotted the street map of Baghdad precisely. When pilots took off they knew their planes' electronic brains could cover the Iraqi capital as well as any taxi driver.

The first combat videos showed a laser-controlled missile hitting an air force HQ in Baghdad with devastating effect. It penetrated a roof ventilator and exploded inside the concrete building. Another film showed a Stealth bomber destroying a defence headquarters and a third showed two 2,000lb bombs blasting straight through the door of a Scud missile storage building.

Already this was becoming a TV war. The commanders in the desert were household names, along with their weapons.

At 7.20am on Saturday, January 19, Saddam's second Scud attack rained down on Tel Aviv as Israelis were debating whether they should leave the relative safety of their gas-proofed homes to visit the synagogue and celebrate the Jewish Sabbath. After three nerve-wrenching false alarms, one triggered by burning debris from a defunct Soviet space craft plunging to Earth, the sirens went off in earnest.

This time Baghdad radio announced that 11 rockets had been launched against the Zionist enemy.

One damaged more than 100 low-rent apartments and another blew a huge crater in one of Tel Aviv's main roads. Sixteen people were injured. The luckiest escape was by a group of 50 mothers and children who had recently come from the Yemen. They had refused to enter the air raid shelter assigned to them, which they claimed was old with vulnerable windows. They insisted on going to another refuge 100 yards away. When the all-clear went an hour later, they emerged into the early morning sunshine to find that the building they had rejected had suffered a direct Scud hit. Only a crater remained.

Once again Daily Expressman Alun Rees was on the spot. Surveying a crater near the city's community theatre, the Mayor of Tel Aviv told him: "Maybe this is like the London blitz. The Windmill Theatre put up a sign which said: We Never Close. I am going to put up such a sign here on this theatre. You can tell the world the show goes on in Tel Aviv."

Hours later the West breathed a sigh of relief when the Israeli Cabinet again decided not to retaliate against Iraq "for the time being".

American Special Forces, backed up by Royal Navy Lynx helicopters, launched a surprise attack against the Iraqi army in the first hand-to-hand battle of the war. The US Delta Force, America's equivalent of the SAS, carried out the raid against

Proud in the face of defeat. Brave Iraqis talk to American marines after being seized at a Kuwaiti oil platform.

Iraqi soldiers occupying nine oil platforms off the Kuwaiti coast. Flying from Allied ships in the Gulf, the raiders destroyed 12 Iraqi units who were using the oil rigs as forward positions to spot Allied planes heading north on round-the-clock bombing missions.

Another 3,500 refugees from Baghdad arrived in Jordan. They were packed into cars wrapped in blankets to protect themselves from the freezing overnight desert temperatures. Egyptian-born Abdul Hamid Mohammed, his wife Zenid and their year-old son Ali had fled from their apartment near the main Rasheed street in central Baghdad.

The 32-year-old tailor said: "When the bombers came it lasted anything from two to six hours. We ran to an underground shelter and stayed there until it was over. The next day many places were damaged, mostly government apartments, although there were many apartments where ordinary people lived. But the people were not hurt because they were sheltering. I love Saddam. We all love Saddam."

Abdul Karim Saleh, a Baghdad taxi driver, described the mood of people in the city. "We have no light or water or telephones, but we do not care. These things are not important," he said. "Bush can kill many of our people but we will eventually crush him like an insect." He ground his foot into the desert sand to reinforce his point.

In Algeria half a million people took to the streets in support of Saddam's fight to expel "the Great Satans from the holy places of Islam." Almost as many turned out in Karachi, Pakistan. In Noakshott, the capital of Mauretania on the Western tip of Africa, police fired tear gas to break up huge pro-Saddam crowds. The anger spread as far away as Manila in the Philippines. Thousands joined "Stop the War" demonstrations in London, including Labour MPs Tony Benn and Ken Livingstone.

Early on Monday, January 21, Iraq launched another blitz, pouring waves of Scud missiles into Riyadh, Dhahran and the Gulf island state of Bahrain from mobile sites in southern Iraq. Most were knocked out by Patriots in spectacular night battles in the Arabian skies.

On the ground swarms of Allied planes attacked the backbone of Saddam's army, the Republican Guard, dug in at bases around northern Kuwait. Saddam's position as leader of Iraq rested to a large extent on their unswerving support for him. Originally formed as an elite force to secure the Baghdad regime from a potential coup, it had grown from eight divisions to 11. Its armoured, mechanised infantry, marines

GENEVA CONVENTION. HOLDING PRISONERS OF WAR AS HUMAN SHIELDS IS FORBIDDEN

The Third Geneva Convention was signed in 1948 and replaced the treaty of the same name which applied during World War Two. It is administered by the International Committee of the Red Cross and forms part of international law. Both Iraq and the allied nations are signatories and have thus agreed to certain basic standards of treatment for POWs.

The captors have to tell the ICRC within a week that they have taken a POW, and the Red Cross then passes on details to the man's family.

The holding of prisoners of war as human shields at defence installations is specifically forbidden. Displaying prisoners at Press conferences or on TV is also ruled out under Article 13, as are public displays or insults.

Captured troops are not obliged to give any other details than basic information – name, rank, serial number, date of birth, nationality. Their captors are allowed to interrogate them to try to gain more but the use of pressure is outlawed.

But interrogation is a valuable tool during a war, and Allied commanders in the Gulf hauled in their Arab linguists for specialist training in interrogation techniques.

The men were trained to grill Iraqi prisoners of war who could provide information to boost intelligence gleaned from US spy satellites, and spies inside Iraq.

Britain's top brass scoured the ranks for Arab speaking officers and sent them on language refresher courses.

The men also had crash courses in interrogating Saddam's front-line soldiers at the Intelligence Corps' training centre in Ashford, Kent.

The Corps' Templer Barracks were the Cold War training ground for hundreds of military spies and intelligence experts. But they were switched from snooping on the Kremlin to grabbing Saddam's military secrets.

One defence source said: "At Templer Barracks they were taught the art of extracting answers from prisoners of war.

"A lot of it is psychological. They had to be able to assess the prisoner's character and judge whether they should be firm with him or butter him up. They were taught how to read body language and all sorts of other vital clues.

"And in Ashford they practiced all they had been taught in confidential surroundings." The linguists served close to any battle frontline with Iraq.

They debriefed the prisoners – giving local commanders a first-hand idea of the forces they were up against.

But the British interrogators were under orders to stand by the Geneva Convention on the rights of POW's – and leave illegal trial by torture to Saddam's military henchmen.

Military analyst Colonel Andrew Duncan said: "Prisoners caught in battle were not likely to help the top brass make their long term plans because they did not know what Saddam is planning. "But on the battlefield it helped officers know precisely what they are up against."

The call to colours for the linguists built on the huge head start the Allies already enjoyed over Iraq in intelligence warfare.

The Americans had about six spy satellites beaming detailed pictures of Saddam's back yard to the Pentagon every day. But Saddam had no access to satellite intelligence.

and special forces brigades possessed the best equipment of the Iraqi army. Many of their officers were trained at Sandhurst.

A WAVE of revulsion swept the civilised world when bruised and exhausted British and American pilots were paraded on Iraqi TV among them Flt Lt Adrian Nichol and Flt Lt John Peters.

Saddam threatened to put all his prisoners of war alongside economic and military targets in an attempt to stop aerial attacks. The pilots, looking gaunt and dejected, were forced to take part in a humiliating TV stunt that broke the rules of the Geneva Convention.

Adrian, standing against a white wall spoke haltingly in a soft voice as he repeated what appeared to be pre-arranged answers to an Iraqi interviewer. These are the words the world heard:

Iraqi voice: What was your mission?

Nichol: To attack an Iraqi oilfield.

Iraqi: Tell us how you have been shot down.

Nichol: I was shot down by an Iraqi system. I do not know what it was.

Iraqi: What do you think of this war against Iraq?

Nichol: I think this war should be stopped so we can go home. I do not agree with this war on Iraq.

Iraqi: Have you a message to be sent?

Nichol: Mum and dad, if you are listening, everything is OK here. Please pray for me. We should be home soon.

The pilots' visible injuries could have been caused when they ejected from their jets, but some military leaders feared that they had been beaten up. Time would soon tell.

John Major expressed his disgust at seeing the captured airmen being paraded on TV. He condemned the holding of hostages at military sites as "inhuman, illegal and contrary to the Geneva Convention."

Under the 1949 Convention, signed by 164 countries including Iraq, prisoners were "entitled in all circumstances to respect for their persons and honour" and had to be protected "against acts of violence or intimidation and against insults or public curiousity."

President Bush said: "America is angry." He warned that Saddam would be made to answer for his crimes after the war and added: "If Saddam thought this brutal treatment of pilots was a way to muster world support, he is dead wrong."

Iraqi diplomats in London and Washington were called in over the propaganda stunt as Baghdad Radio accused the captured fliers of

committing their own war crimes by bombing "civilian, economic and educational targets and killing and injuring civilians."

Behind the war of words and the suffering of men and women in the front line on both sides, was the agony of the servicemen's families in Britain who watched every TV news bulletin, read every newspaper and waited.

For the families of Adrian and John, their TV appearances offered hope. Adrian's parents John and Catherine Nichol heard their son's voice on a CNN broadcast from Baghdad shortly before midnight on Sunday January 20, London time. The couple, who had waited for news of their missing son behind the closed curtains of their home, wept and hugged each other with joy in the living room.

"My son is alive, my son is alive! Our prayer is answered!" shouted Mr Nichol. By morning their joy had again turned to anguish with the news that Adrian had been moved to a military target. "Now we are praying that the Iraqis follow the Geneva Convention," Mr Nichol said.

The mother of Flt Lt John Peters, after seeing newspaper pictures of her son's face said: "He looks pretty bad, but at least he is alive."

Brian and Kay Peters had stayed by the TV while news bulletins showed Adrian. But in those first few hours all they had heard was a tape of John's voice, giving his name rank and number.

There was grief for the families of other Tornado pilots missing but not pictured by the Iraqis. They could only fear the worst.

The Government won a massive majority of 529 votes by MPs in support of the war. A handful of Labour rebels including Social Security

Face of war that shocked Britain: Pilot John Peters who appeared on Iraqi television.

spokesman Tony Banks and veteran Left-winger Bob Cryer denied the Government unanimous backing with the final figures 563 for and 34 against the motion expressing: "full support for British Forces in the Gulf and their contribution to the implementation of the United Nations resolutions by the multinational armies."

The unprecedented degree of cross-party backing came after a 6-hour debate in which John Major warned Britain to brace itself for a long and painful war.

Saddam rejected a peace proposal from Soviet President Mikhail Gorbachev, saying it should be sent to Washington. Defence Secretary Tom King launched a Gulf Trust for public donations to families of servicemen killed or injured in the Gulf. American stars including Meryl Streep and Shirley MacLaine refused to fly to London for the premiere of their movie Postcards From The Edge, because of terrorist fears. The Jockey Club announced it was inundated with calls from owners wanting to name racehorses Desert Storm, insurance bills for aircraft and shipping bound for the Middle East soared because of Iraqi missile risks, and American actress Margot Kidder, 41, who played Lois Lane in the Superman films, climbed from a wheelchair to speak at an anti-war protest in New York. Weeping Margot, paralysed in a movie accident, said: "Saddam Hussein is a monster but the ultimate Human Rights abuse is war. It's the Bush administration, and only the Bush administration, that brought this on."

On Tuesday January 21, Israel suffered its bloodiest attack yet from Iraq. Scores of Israelis were buried alive before they could be rescued and three old people died of heart attacks when Scud missiles again rained down on Tel Aviv. A women lost both legs after a building collapsed and 20 homes in three blocks were blown away. Two Scuds fell harmlessly short of their targets.

Patriot missiles were fired to repel the attacks. "But they did not hit," said Brigadier General Nachman Shai of the Israeli Army. "They will hit the next time, I hope, if there is a next time. We are at war here."

Had Saddam pushed the Israelis too far this time? John Major denounced the "repugnant attack" and President Bush again appealed to Israel not to retaliate. The Israeli government's patience was at breaking point as rescue workers dug with bare hands to reach people trapped in the debris. The same things were happening in Baghdad and other Iraqi cities.

Saddam's armed might lay deep beneath the sand. His forces, including Russian-built tanks and MiG fighters, were hidden in Western-designed shelters tougher than anything

in Europe and America, with reinforced roofs more than a metre thick and sliding 40-ton doors.

More Allied pilots were paraded on TV. Saddam's Republican Guard was reported to have set Kuwait's Al Wafra oilfield ablaze to hinder the laser-guided missiles homing in on them.

John Major asked for a massive cash boost from Britain's allies to avert a rise in taxes to meet the bill for the Gulf War. He attacked some of Britain's European Community partners for not playing a bigger part in the war effort. The first four days of the conflict had already cost Britain £100 million. Mr Major urged nations like Japan, Germany and Belgium to do more. Both Germany and Japan were restrained by their constitutions from directly taking part in the war. The German government had at this time given £1.5 billion to the war effort and Japan had pledged £2 billion.

ONTROVERSY began to surround the one Western TV network allowed to remain in Iraq, CNN or Chicken Network News, as it was becoming nicknamed. The world was craving for Gulf War news and CNN had seized a huge slab of the market with gripping picture reports from newsmen under missile attack.

"CNN scores a coup as TV dramatically captures the first major war in the era of instant worldwide communication," said Time magazine. But the question was being asked: At what price? Rival US networks and the British media were perturbed that CNN seemed to be so well in with with the Iraqi authorities. Was CNN guilty of stage-managing the news? On-camera staffers were urged to don gas masks even for interviews, raising the emotional temperature. Pictures showing devastation to allegedly civilian areas began coming out of Iraq.

CNN never offered analysis of the news. It offered the excitement and danger of the moment. Its approach was popular with viewers, but not with President Bush. He believed that Saddam was using CNN as his mouthpiece in the propaganda war.

The White House was incensed over the reporting of what the Iraqis claimed was a bombed baby milk factory. CNN reporter Peter Arnett was taken to the ruins by Iraqi Ministry of Information minders. He told of salvage teams carrying sacks of powdered milk from the shattered building and suggested that Allied bombers had blundered. The Iraqis said the £75 million plant was the country's only source of milk powder for babies under a year old.

US military officials retaliated during a briefing at their High Command in Riyadh.

Taciturn air force spokesman Lt Col Mike Gallagher shuffled satellite pictures and asked: "If this was a baby milk plant, how come it had Iraqi troops swarming all over it? Military guards were all around a barbed wire fence. There was a military garrison outside and numerous sources indicated that the facility was associated with biological warfare production."

Asked if his statements meant that CNN reports were incorrect, he retorted: "Sounds good to me."

There was more controversy when Germany admitted that some of its companies had broken UN sanctions and sold gas and biological warfare weapon components to Iraq. Economic minister Juergen Moellmann confessed that Germany had supplied Saddam with war materials in spite of the trade embargo. More than 100 firms were said to be involved. He also admitted that German technicians may have helped Iraq refine the Soviet-made Scud B missiles it was using against Israel and Saudi Arabia. Moellmann pledged that investigators would probe the suspect companies involved.

As Patriot missiles successfully knocked down continuing Scud attacks on Dhahran, Riyadh and Tel Aviv, it was revealed that two Iraqi peasants had been paid £15,000 for handing over a British airman to Baghdad. Tornado navigator Flt Lt Robert Stewart, 44, was shot down with his pilot, Flt Lt David Waddington, at 24, the youngest flyer in the force. Wounded and shaken, Flt Lt Stewart was overpowered by two Arabs who handed him over to the army and collected their bounty. Flt Lt Waddington, who was also believed to have ejected, was listed as missing in action.

In Britain sales of Union Jacks soared at the family firm of Mott and Jones in Swansea. Two Moslem taxi drivers who displayed posters of Saddam in Doncaster were attacked by passers-by.

The Allied air offensive continued unabated. General Colin Powell went on television to assure Americans that Operation Desert Storm was on course for victory. It was another relaxed and polished performance from America's top soldier. It came at an opportune time, for President Bush was clearly worried by reports that the Allied war machine was missing its targets. "We are not bogged down," said Powell. "Saddam has not thrown back a single military punch." He displayed intelligence photographs of Allied strikes and added: "I don't want to give too much away because Saddam might be watching me. But trust me, it's real good."

US Defence Secretary Dick Cheney, alongside, said: "The general is right. Saddam will quit long before we will. Each day that goes by he gets weaker and we get stronger. I noticed a newspaper headline that said: War Drags On. Please understand that war cannot be scored like a college track meet or a baseball tournament."

The euphoria of the first spectacular air strikes was receding, and reaction was setting in. The military men and the politicians were at pains to point out that this was no Hollywood war, over in an evening. This was hard pounding against a strong, well-armed and ruthless enemy. This was the real thing.

Three Iraqi jets were shot down in a dogfight seconds before they could launch an Exocet missile attack against British ships in the Gulf. The French-built Mirages carrying the Exocets, scourge of the Royal Navy during the Falklands war, and a Russian-made MiG 23 guarding them, emerged from hiding and flew towards their targets. A Saudi pilot on air combat patrol in his F-15 Eagle fighter answered the alert from the Navy warships. Millions of TV viewers heard him shout "Bandit! Bandit!" as he swept in for the kill. He destroyed both Mirages in mid-air with Sidewinder missiles as the MiG fled for home. "I did it for my country," Captain Ayedh said later. RAF jets let the MiG escape, tracking it back to its base...which was later visited by Tornado bombers.

In another confrontation, Allied forces gained a toehold on Kuwaiti soil after a fierce skirmish with Iraqi troops. The island of Qarawah, 40 miles north-east of the Saudi border, was taken when Allied forces backed by a Royal Navy Lynx helicopter from HMS Cardiff chased two Iraqi

Baby milk factory or biological warfare plant? The war of words raged over this Baghdad bombing

minesweepers along the Kuwaiti coastline. One of the minesweepers struck an Iraqi mine as she ran. The other was sunk by American air attack. The Allies then came under heavy fire from the island and replied with bombs. US marines stormed ashore. Twenty two Iraqi sailors were pulled from the water and another 20 were captured on the island. Three died.

It was a significant moment. This was the first piece of Kuwaiti territory to be liberated from the invaders and jubilant Kuwaiti troops hoisted their national flag over the island once more.

Two of Iraq's nuclear reactors were knocked out at Tuatha near Baghdad. It was announced that Britain's air power in the Gulf was to be reinforced by Buccaneer strike aircraft from RAF Lossiemouth in north-east Scotland. The 1960s-vintage Buccaneers were among the oldest planes still in service with the RAF, but they were equipped with laser bomb-guidance systems to aid the Tornado strikes and carried a powerful punch in their own right.

A minor piece of naval history was made when a US Los Angeles class submarine fired Tomahawk cruise missiles from beneath the surface of the Red Sea, the first time Tomahawks had been launched from a submerged vessel. Their targets were Iraqi chemical weapons plants. A previously-secret weapon, the Stand-off Land Attack Missile (SLAM) was fired from a battleship off the Gulf shores. A camera in the missile's nose-cone relayed pictures of the target looming closer and closer until the second of impact. Saddam's navy came under heavy bombardment at Basra. Iraqi prisoners of war, covered in lice and sores, revealed that they had

been lucky to get one meal a day.

In the desert, CBS-TV reporter Bob Simons and three companions went missing. A Saudi patrol found their car abandoned on the Kuwaiti border where they had gone to film front-line troops digging in.

ADDAM, apparently unable to make any kind of military impression on the Allies, declared war on a softer target, the wildlife of the Gulf. Millions of gallons of crude oil started pouring into the sea from the Kuwaiti tanker terminal of Mina al-Ahmadi. The Iraqi leader had ordered the pumps switched on, for what reason nobody could quite work out. The move had little military significance. It seemed to be an act of pure spite. The slick, 30 miles long and eight miles wide, started drifting down the Gulf.

President Bush described the act as environmental terrorism. Prince Abdul Aziz, oil adviser to King Fahd, declared: "Saddam is the father of destruction." The slick was already twelve times the size of the 1989 Exxon Valdez tanker spillage when 10 million gallons of oil flooded on to the coast of Alaska, causing an ecological disaster. The Kuwaiti oil threatened another. Environmentalists were particularly concerned about the effect on the Gulf's dolphins, seabirds, turtles and coral. Stricken birds were already floundering and dying in the slick. There was also a threat to shoreline trees such as carab and mangrove.

The oil drifted closer to the desalination plants providing fresh water from the sea along the coasts of Saudi Arabia, Qatar, Bahrain and the United Arab Emirates. Giant floating booms were thrown around the plants to keep the slick from the intakes. British pollution experts flew to the Gulf with 90 tons of the best equipment available. More booms were placed around islands in the narrow waterways where green turtles had their breeding grounds and the local variety of sea cow, the dugong, could seek refuge. Tanks full of living coral were flown from the Gulf to the waters of the Red Sea.

The Allied reply was swift. A US F1-11 jet fired two TV-guided precision GBU15 bombs at oil pipe manifolds at Mina al Ahmadi, cutting the gush of oil to a trickle.

In Saudi Arabia claims that the Tornado crews' performance was poor were fiercely rejected by their chief, Group Captain David Henderson. He said he was sick and tired of the knocking, which was causing distress to the crewmen's families. Henderson was angered by remarks made by retired US Air Force General Sam Perry, who had

Innocent victim of war: An oil-stricken Gulf seabird fights for survival on the shore

described the RAF's performance during the blitz on Iraq as disappointing. Henderson said on TV: "I am sick of people talking about Tornado mission failures. That sort of language makes ME very disappointed. We have been very, very effective out there."

The effectiveness of the Iraqi air force was zero, more than 100 of their aircraft cut and run to Iran. Among them were the cream of Saddam's pilots with their Mirage F-15s, MiG 29 Fulcrums, MiG 23 Floggers, SU-24 Fencer bombers and 30 transport and civilian aircraft. Teheran said some of the planes were damaged when they arrived. At least two crashed. Few had their weapons. Iran, underlining its neutrality in the conflict, said the jets would stay where they were until hostilities ceased.

This meant that the Allies had almost total dominance of the skies. But both the White House and Downing Street were puzzled as to the motive behind the mass defections, which left Saddam's ground forces dangerously exposed. Was the Iraqi leader mothballing his planes until after the conflict, so he had an air force that would live to fight another day or rather live to fight one day, since it had hardly fought at all? No one could say.

The Allies were further boosted when 30 Iraqi troops defending an island surrendered to US forces. Demoralised and malnourished, they marked out a misspelt message SOS, "we serrender" in stones on a beach at Unn al-Maradin, 15 miles east of the Kuwaiti port of Mina Azzahr.

Polls in Britain revealed that John Major was the most popular Prime Minister since Winston Churchill. His calm, unfussed approach to the crisis had won him many friends and his popularity outstripped even that of Mrs Thatcher during the height of the Falklands war.

Labour leader Neil Kinnock, by contrast, was facing a damaging front-bench rebellion over his support for the Gulf War. Firebrand Left-winger Clare Short and others feared that Kinnock was under pressure to widen the war aims once Saddam withdrew from Kuwait. Britain would be "sucked into a war aim that meant bombarding Iraq" she warned. "That would be a serious error."

Other anti-war protestors took things further. A bomb exploded outside the offices of the Liberation newspaper in Paris, injuring three watchmen. Terrorists bombed the American consulate in the Turkish city of Adana, close to the Nato airbase at Interlik. No one was hurt. Three Moslem protestors were shot dead in Pakistan as pro-Saddam demonstrations swept the country. Saddam was promising martyrdom to those dying in worldwide "commando attacks"

D-day in the dunes: A column of military vehicles regroup near the Kuwaiti border hours after the start of the land war

on Allied nations and their interests.

With Britain now spending £3.6 million a day on the war, the pressure was on to raise yet more cash from European allies.

The figures illustrating the cost of the campaign began to defy description. One armoured division of 350 US Abrams tanks was using more than 600,000 gallons of fuel a day nearly twice the consumption of General Patton's entire Third Army as it drove across France in 1944. The US was serving a million meals a day. More prosaically, but just as necessary, a daily consignment of 600 lavatories, 200 showers and 100 wash basins were being dispatched to the sands of Saudi Arabia. All that was being transported in 250 ships, 100 of which were at sea at any one time. Military and civilian planes flying in supplies had already completed 7,000 missions, among their cargo 500,000 camouflaged condoms to keep the sand out of British rifle barrels.

Japan, which ran on Gulf oil, promised £4.8 billion to help finance the war. Several EC countries moved to deflect criticism from Britain's Defence Minister, Alan Clark, that the prosperous nations of Europe had responded to the crisis by "running to their cellars". Belgium, reviled for refusing to even sell ammunition to Britain, suddenly offered the US £1.4 billion and 1,000 M269 automatic weapons.

Day in, day out, the Allied pounding went on. Royal Navy helicopters destroyed an Iraqi sabotage flotilla in the Gulf. The Iraqi army was also hit when US marines and Allied bombers ambushed a convoy in the Kuwaiti desert, wrecking 24 tanks plus armoured vehicles and personnel carriers.

Iraq claimed that a captured Allied pilot had been killed after being held at a prime bombing

Missing Melissa: The first American woman soldier ever taken in battle

target. John Major was appalled by the Baghdad Radio report. Britain's Gulf commander, General Sir Peter de la Billiere, said of Saddam: "The value of human life is of no consequence to him." Both Britain and the US called in Iraqi diplomats and condemned the treatment of captured servicemen. Foreign Office minister Douglas Hogg reported that Iraq's ambassador to Britain, Dr Azmi al-Salihi, appeared "singularly ignorant" when asked about the treatment of British POWs. "His reply was not persuasive he sort of mumbled," said Mr Hogg. "He was very downcast. He left even more downcast."

French defence minister Jean-Pierre Chevenement quit after his troops in Saudi Arabia admitted morale was low. Soldiers risked reprisals to go on TV and complain of poor food and lack of water. They questioned why they had been sent to fight Saddam. Their reservations reflected Chevenement's own reluctance to fight. The Left-winger had opposed the sending of the 12,000-strong French contingent, which included elements of the fearsome Foreign Legion. Chevenement, who had helped to found the Franco-Iraq Friendship Committee, had been expecting the sack from President Mitterrand. He jumped before he was pushed, claiming that France was now involved beyond its commitment to simply liberate Kuwait.

AT MIDNIGHT on Tuesday January 29, as a full moon hung over the desert and temperatures dropped close to freezing, the Iraqi army made a bold attempt to lure the Allies into a ground war. A hundred Iraqi troops in five tanks and a number of armoured personnel carriers drove through the sands towards the almost deserted Saudi border town of Khafji. The small force clashed with an advance unit of US Marines and came under heavy artillery, machine gun and rocket fire.

As the surprised Allies responded in a battle that raged for 12 hours, more than 4,000 Iraqi troops and 100 Russian-built T-53 tanks crossed the Saudi border to within range of the oil town of Al-Wafra, further west. The tanks advanced with their gun turrets facing backwards, a signal that they wished to surrender. As Allied forces watched, the turrets swivelled round and opened fire on the Saudi positions.

In Khafji, the Iraqis were advancing into the outskirts of the town. A US Marines reconnaisance team called in Cobra helicopters and A10 ground attack jets to engage them. As darkness fell again after a day of battle the sky was lit up by explosions. The night echoed to the sound of diving aircraft, tank fire and the rattle of machine guns. There was some ugly street fighting. Brave Iraqis trapped in the resort town were reported to be fighting to the death.

The US lost its first casualties on the ground. Twelve marines died and two were wounded. Tragically, seven marines died from so-called friendly fire after a missile from one of their own planes destroyed their armoured troop carrier.

But hundreds of Iraqi troops were killed and 41 of their tanks destroyed. Helicopter pilots told of burning vehicles littering the desert. Fifty Iraqi tanks were trapped in their own minefields as they tried to flee back across the border. Allied convoys raced to reinforce the area against reports that more of Saddam's troops were massing on the border backed by 1,000 tanks.

A handful of Iraqis briefly took over an abandoned holiday hotel, the Khafji Beach, but they were routed. There was one bizarre incident when two invaders answered the hotel telephone. "We are Iraqi soldiers, who are you?" one asked, while the other put in: "We are with Saddam, with Arabism." When they realised the caller was Egyptian one shouted: "See you in Jerusalem!" and hung up.

Baghdad Radio announced that Saddam had personally supervised the attack and claimed that Iraq had routed the Allied forces. "The army of Saddam Hussein is wiping out the renegade invaders and knocking out the forces of infidelism, corruption and treason," it trumpeted. "The vanguards of victory are levelling the positions of the forces of the tyrants in Khafji."

Iraq assured the Saudis that the advance should not be interpreted as an invasion attempt. "Our entry into your land is not an occupation, but is made necessary by the circumstances of the fight against the armies of atheism and aggression that have turned your land into a base for aggression," Baghdad Radio added in characteristic tautological style.

After suffering weeks of merciless bombardment the Iraqi tank crews had been required to embroil the Allies in an all-out land battle before coalition commanders were ready for it. It did not work. And General Schwarzkopf was scathing about the occupation of Khafji. "If you walk into an uninhabited place it is not much of a seizure," he said. He denied that the Arab forces guarding the front had been taken by surprise by the combat-hardened Iraqis. And asked about the number of Iraqi dead he said: "We are in the business of shooting them, not counting them."

He did not think Saddam's army was about to give in. He was right. As he spoke more slow-moving columns of Iraqi armour lumbered from their holes in the sand and headed for the

Saudi border. They came under ferocious attack from Allied fighter-bombers. Baghdad Radio now claimed that Saddam was personally marshalling his troops on the southern front.

Allied commanders were puzzled by the move. The six Iraqi divisions had no air cover and there were almost too many targets to choose from. Hundreds of planes including B-52 bombers and British and French Jaguars pounded the Iraqi formations. "It was almost like you flipped on the kitchen light at night and the cockroaches started scurrying," said Lt Col Dick "Snake" White, the commander of an American Harrier jump-jet squadron.

Inevitably, the first land battle of the war ended in catastrophic losses for Iraq. But there was little satisfaction in it for the Allies. It was a massacre, leaving the desert stained with blood.

As the desert armies mopped up London announced that American B-52s were to fly missions direct from RAF Fairford in Gloucestershire. They would carpet-bomb targets in Iraq and Kuwait on regular 14-hour missions. British troops in the Gulf had something to celebrate with a 12.2 per cent pay rise, well above inflation. An army private's pay rose from a basic £6,665 to £7,466. A brigadier went from £42,358 to £50,003.

The victory at Khafji was overshadowed by the capture of an American woman soldier the first ever taken in battle. An old oak tree in the town of Newaygo, Michigan, was festooned with yellow ribbons for 20-year-old Melissa Rathbun-Nealy.

Her parents, Leo and Joan, had paid little attention to the initial Pentagon announcement saying a woman soldier was missing. "At first, we thought that surely out of hundreds of women stationed in Saudi Arabia the girl wouldn't be our daughter," said Leo.

But they learned that Melissa, their only daughter had disappeared with 24-year-old transport battalion colleague David Lockett. Their jeep was found abandoned in the desert with their duffel bags and gas masks still in the vehicle. The jeep has got lost, then stuck, then came under fire.

Melissa's feared fate contrasted with that of another female combatant. First woman deserter of the Gulf War, reserve doctor Yolande Huet-Vaughan, 39, gave herself up after speaking at a rally in Missouri. British deserter, Lance Bombadier Vic Williams, who fled from the Germany-based Royal Artillery 27th Field Regiment the day before he was due to leave for the Gulf, addressed an anti-war rally in Hyde Park.

Early in February, the 16-inch guns of "Mighty Mo", the American Second World War Battleship Missouri, which could hit a target the size of a tennis court from 20 miles, pounded Iraq's forces in Kuwait. It was the first time a naval bombardment had been ordered on shore installations.

Prime Minister John Major warned his War Cabinet the ground was being prepared for the land battle as planes dropped a bomb a minute on Iraq and Saddam claimed the Allies were targetting civilians.

President Bush revealed he wept every time an American serviceman was killed in battle. "We have had very few losses, but I feel every one of them," he said. And a distressed Kuwaiti pilot told how he could see his home on the horizon as he bombed an Iraqi target.

Saddam was still defiant. There was no sign of peace. The Iraqi leader vowed President Bush would be hunted by Iraqi assassins for the rest of

Front line force: Saudi tanks roll down the highway to Khafji, scene of the first major land battle

his life in a chilling broadcast on Baghdad Radio. Premier John Major was also on Saddam's wanted list and security around leading British politicians was stepped up.

Baghdad Radio accused Mr Bush of trying to bomb Iraq out of existance, and ordered the severing of diplomatic ties with the U.S., Britain, France, Spain, Egypt and Saudi Arabia. King Hussein of Jordan called on Arabs to demand a ceasefire in the Gulf. Hours later Prime Minister John Major and his War Cabinet escaped death by a few feet in an IRA mortar bomb attack on No. 10. The shell, blasted through a hole cut in the roof of a van parked in Whitehall, landed in the back garden, rocking the building and shattering reinforced windows. The rocket, directed at a Cabinet room was deflected when it hit a cherry tree. Two other bombs overshot their target and landed in nearby Horse Guard's Parade. They failed to explode properly.

Britain was snowbound. Road, rail and air services were crippled. The country shivered to a standstill. But still the war in the Gulf was on everyone's lips. When would the land battle begin? The best news was that the nation's 40,000 troops in the Gulf were to be given nearly £1 million worth of free telephone calls home.

Meanwhile hopes were high that Britain would win a major share in £20 billion plans to rebuild Kuwait after the State's exiled leaders met 10 top UK businessmen ... from banking, construction, engineering and planning. Britain had constructed much of Kuwait in the 50s and 60s and still held plans for many bombed installations. That day, thousands of angry viewers accused the BBC of sounding as if it was using propaganda scripts written by Saddam Hussein. They jammed the Corporation's Lime Grove switchboard to protest at the Nine O'Clock news bulletin on the bombing of Baghdad. It showed tragic pictures of injured Iraqi civilians after a raid on the city's outskirts. Allied commanders said the attack was against a military command centre, but Baghdad claimed the bombers hit a public air raid shelter, killing up to 600 civilians. Angry Tory MPs called on the BBC to withdraw their correspondents from Iraq. The BBC announced: "We make it clear that broadcasts from Baghdad are censored."

The Americans insisted there was no mistake by the two Stealth bomber pilots. They picked up military signals from the bunker.

Commanders in the Gulf "deeply regretted the civilian losses." Terry Gander, Editor of Jane's NBC Protection Yearly revealed Iraq had built air-raid shelters with army command centres in civilian areas.

As the war of words raged Syria's strongman President Aafez Assad raised hopes of a long-term Middle East peace settlement. It appeared the nation might be willing to recognise Israel's right to exist.

The surprise offer by President Assad emerged after talks in Damascus between German Foreign Minister Hans-Dietrich Genscher and his Syrian opposite number Farouk al-Sharaa.

The Germans promised Israel £50 million to buy U.S. Patriot Missiles as part of Chancellor Helmut Kohl's £330 million package of military and economic aid for the war.

The bombing of Iraq and its troops in the Kuwait sand increased and the music of Bruce Springsteen and Meatloaf became America's new weapon. U.S. marines crept within a mile of the Kuwaiti border and set up 1,000 watt speaker stacks. They trailed wires back to their bunkers and blasted the Iraqi troops with rock 'n' roll.

Sadly Britain lost its seventh Tornado bomber. The two-man crew, listed as missing went down as they prepared to fire laser-guided missiles.

Meanwhile, Labour leader Neil Kinnock sacked his junior Social Security spokeswoman, Clare Short, for again publicly questioning his backing of the Gulf War. She feared the bombing of Iraq was starting to go beyond the war aims set out by the UN.

With the clock ticking towards a land battle there was one last hope for peace. It came from Soviet leader Mikhail Gorbachev who met Iraqi Foreign Minister Tariq Aziz in Moscow.

Their talks were scheduled to take two days but lasted just 3.5 hours after pressure from the Allies. Mr Gorbachev had asked Mr Bush for more time to conjure up a peace plan...but he was given just 36 hours. After that the Allied tanks would roll into Kuwait.

Mr Aziz arrived back in Baghdad as the capital received one of its fiercest poundings by bombers since the outbreak of war and British and American troops massed for a final showdown. On his way he had stopped off in Teheran for talks with Iran's President Rafsanjani and admitted that his nation was seriously thinking of pulling out of Kuwait. For the first time he conceded that 20,000 Iraqis had now been killed and 60,000 wounded. Two hundred tanks a day were being knocked out and at least a third of Iraq's armour was destroyed.

Downing Street and the White House were "cool" over the Soviet peace initiative. One controversial point was a pledge that there would be no more sanctions against Baghdad and Iraq could keep its "state structures" and borders after

its withdrawal. This meant Saddam would retain what was left of his military machine. And the plan did not give any adequate guarantees about the future security of Kuwait after the war.

The Allies had now decided there could be no peace talks while Saddam was in power and they wanted his war machine dismantled.

The Iraqi leader meanwhile did not seem to grasp the urgency of giving the Russians, or the UN, a speedy reply to the initiative. As the Allied deadline for a land war neared, Baghdad Radio announced that the Ruling Revolutionary Council would send Mr Aziz back to Moscow "sometime soon."

The Kremlin stressed they needed an immediate reply to their proposals. An Aeroflot jet had been laid on to pick up Mr Aziz and they would even accept a telex. Soviet officials tried hard to swallow their anger and impatience as Iraq's ambassador to the UN Abdul Admir al-Anbari announced his government was in the process of "finalising its response."

As he spoke, Baghdad Radio vowed to fight to the end and Iraqi Information Minister Latif Jassem dared Allied commander General Schwarzkopf "to try his luck on the battlefield." Saturation bombings by the Allies reached 2,900 sorties and another 28 Iraqi tanks were destroyed.

Finally Mr Aziz did return to the Soviet Union. But as he walked across the tarmac at Moscow Airport to deliver his answer to the Russian peace plan, Saddam gave the world his reply.

Two hundred Kuwaiti oil wells were set on fire as the Iraqi leader made a 30-minute speech on Baghdad Radio pledging he would never surrender. Again he claimed Iraq would win "the Mother of Battles."

He told his nation: "They want us to surrender but they will be disappointed. They do not want us to withdraw. They want to strip Iraq of all power. There is no other course except the one of humiliation and darkness. The Iraqis continue to ask and work for what will make them more brilliant, faithful and lofty."

As his words faded the Desert Rats joined with other Allied artillery to stage the most violent land barrage since the Second World War. Mr Aziz hastily negotiated with the Kremlin on a new six-point plan that gave Iraq 21 days after a ceasefire to get out of Kuwait, supervised by a UN force. But now the White House laid down its tough terms for surrender. They included: Total withdrawal within 24 hours-by 5pm UK time on Saturday February 23; all POWs released within 48 hours and Kuwait's exiled rulers allowed back in their country within two days.

To underline their resolve, U.S. jets dropped napalm into the fuel filled moats Iraq had set up in front of its positions.

The deadline came and went. The Kuwaiti oil wells blazed and Saddam fired a Scud missile at Israel. Then, just like that fateful day on August 2, 1990 the still of the desert was broken by a roar, dust swirled in the darkness and hundreds of tanks lumbered from their holes in the sand and headed for Kuwait City.

It was the point of no return for the Allies. The Mother of Destiny was with them.

Baghdad war room. Saddam briefs his generals. The Kremlin had put forward a peace plan but the war went on

CHAPTER 8

THE GULF WAR

'We are going around, over, through, on top, underneath and any other way it takes to beat them.'

General Schwarzkopf

One last order from General Stormin' Norman Schwarzkopf launched the land battle to free Kuwait City: "Knock 'em hard, knock 'em fast and knock 'em OUT:" he said. As his words echoed over the 50ft square map-lined Riyadh war room inside Saudi Arabia's white concrete Ministry of Defence, the mood was one of determination...and relief that the waiting was over. The commanders left to undertake their task. They were part of a precise-timing battle plan that when printed out on computer paper, stood more than two feet high.

Beside General Schwarzkopf was a telephone with an open line to the White House allowing President Bush to stop the attack at any time. It stayed silent.

The General had drawn a circle around February 24 on his calender for the land battle. He picked 1am GMT just before dawn in the Gulf, for H-hour as the Generals called it. When the moon would throw no light over the Iraqi troops. They would be blinded without the night-sight

devices of the 28-nation Alliance against them.

The date gave time to complete at least the heaviest fighting of Saddam's "Mother of Wars," before the sand storms came and the daytime heat turned the desert into an open oven. It also avoided the holy month of Ramadan which started on March 17. Though some great Islamic battles had been fought in that month, many believed Saddam would use the presence of infidels on Holy Lands at that time as a propaganda weapon.

As daylight broke over the desert, the armies of more than a million men were locked in the battle the world prayed would not happen.

The battered but proud people of Baghdad woke to the shattering news. Some stunned residents gathered on street corners of the bombed city, listening in confused silence to their transistor radios as Saddam urged his nation to "fight them and show no mercy ... fight, fight, fight the infidel."

Many of his people had been led to believe they were on the brink of peace and that Saddam

92

would emerge with some kind of victory from the war. Broadcasts repeated by Baghdad Radio had told of Iraq's acceptance of the Soviet plan for a ceasefire but ignored the Allied rejection. Now news of the ground assault was a massive blow to the citizens who already had no electricity, gas, petrol and little clean water.

All through the day, announcers claimed Iraqi troops were inflicting heavy casualties on the enemy. They had contained the assault and burned hundreds of tanks and personnel carriers.

In reality it was another story.

When H-hour came the Allies imposed a news blackout as coalition forces, wearing full chemical protective gear, broke through Iraqi sand barriers with giant bulldozers to create an Invasion Alley.

Challenger tanks of Britain's 4th and 7th Armoured Brigades raced through minefields 60 miles into Iraq with orders to seek and destroy the Republican Guards' Soviet-built T72 tanks around Basra, the nation's second city. The 8,000 men who had been taking anti-nerve and anti-anthrax pills for days, knew they had the most dangerous mission of the war. Alongside them were French Legionnaires and the U.S. 7th Army with its Abrams.

Their two commanding officers, Brigadier

Christopher Hammerbeck and Brigadier Patrick Cordingley, joined the charge in the turrets of their own tanks. The speed of the advance left the Iraqi troops reeling.

The weather was far from perfect with low cloud and strong winds whipping into the faces of tank commanders roaring to their final battle positions.

Small teams of SAS and U.S. Special Forces, disguised as Arabs were activated on hit and run missions behind enemy lines. Some had been in Baghdad for months. They marked pre-arranged sites with laser pistols before an air raid. The U.S. battleships Wisconsin and Missouri edged closer to Kuwait under cover of darkness, after British minesweepers cleared their paths. Before sunrise they were bombarding the coastline and off-shore islands still held by the Iraqis, who expected an amphibious landing.

B52 bombers and the RAF's Tornado GR-1s and F-16A fighter bombers struck designated targets around Basra. But the honour of being first across the border went to the Kuwaiti army. Their handful of tanks backed up by the U.S. 2nd Marine Division, smashed through the front door to Kuwait City advancing straight up the main coastal highway.

Cobra helicopters threw a protective shield over them destroying any Iraqi tank that showed a turret. The spearhead force, that also included Saudi and Egyptian troops, smashed through razor wire, sand ramparts and burning oil pits that Saddam had claimed would "devour the infidels."

The Kuwaiti army was finally going home. It was a just reward for the teachers, architects, civil servants and lawyers who had signed up to fight for their little country. Puffing cigarettes, laughing and waving, they weren't afraid of dying as they charged through the desert knowing they would soon, hopefully see their families.

It took just 10 hours for the massive Allied Army to conquer ground they expected to take over days. Ten thousand Iraqi prisoners were quickly taken and thousands more, dazed and battered after 38 days of the most intensive bombing in history, streamed from their sand holes carrying white flags. Some even kissed their captors, relieved their ordeal was over.

Morale was high. "They call them the elite Republican Guards. They won't be so bloody elite when they meet the Royal Jocks!" a Sergeant of the Royal Scots, the oldest regiment in the British Army told Daily Express reporter Bill Greig.

General Schwarzkopf held a briefing to announce: "We are going to go around, over, through, on top, underneath and any other way it takes to beat them." But he cautioned: "I would not be honest with you if I didn't remind you

Surrender: A column of Iraqi prisoners of war on the first day of the land war. They had endured weeks of bombing. Peace for all troops on both sides was near

these are very early stages."

The only real response to the Allied attack came in Kuwait City. Iraqi troops blew up its landmarks. The parliament building, the Emir's palace and Bayan conference centre were badly hit, along with four top hotels ... the Sheraton Meridian, Plaza and Marriot. The tiny kingdom's liberating troops could see the pall of smoke shrouding the city as they seized the town of Jahra ...a crossroads, 25 miles to the west. Up to 200 oil wells were also blazing.

s the Allied noose tightened, Baghdad Radio announced that Saddam had ordered his troops to pull out of Kuwait. A statement said: "The Iraqi leadership had stressed its acceptance to withdraw in accordance with UN Security Council Resolution 660 when it agreed to the Soviet peace proposal.

"In compliance with this decision, orders were issued to the armed forces for an organised withdrawal to the positions in which they were before the August 1, 1990!"

It was a ray of hope. But the statement did not give a time frame for the withdrawal.

That same evening 28 American soldiers were killed and scores wounded in the Gulf's most devastating Scud attack. The 1,000lb missiles slammed into an army barracks just outside Dhahran. No Patriot missiles had been launched because the Scud was already disintegrating over the city. But it sent down a shower of debris, including the warhead. Among the dead were two women reservists ... the first American troops to die in the war.

As the Soviet Union presented yet another peace plan to the United Nations, proposing that the Security Council set a date for the start of an Iraqi withdrawal, the Desert Rats hit Saddam's Republican Guard hard. Thirty five of the elite troops' T-75s were destroyed in southern Iraq. At the same time 80 other Soviet-built tanks from the 150,000 strong force were moved south to dodge the British closing in behind them.

America's crack Screaming Eagles were flown into battle by women pilots in the biggest helicopter assault ever launched. The Chinooks, Blackhawks, Hueys, Cobras and Apaches helped ferry two thousand paratroopers and supplies of the 101st Airborne Division deep into Iraq. Dust from the three hundred helicopters turned the sky purple as they came together from 13 bases, carving out a 60-square-mile fuel dump.

As night fell on Day Two of the land offensive, the Desert Rats were sweeping deeper into Iraq and towards the Euphrates river. The pride of Saddam's army was virtually cut off. French

troops had forced their way 100 miles into Iraq, capturing 3,000 men and severing supply and communication lines to the Guards. All the way along the Front, entire Iraqi battalions were waving white flags. Now more than 20,000 had surrendered. Still thousands more, exhausted, cold and hungry, were giving up, threatening to slowdown the Allied advance. Over 300 tanks, one every six minutes had been destroyed and Allied troops had encircled Kuwait City.

At sea a radar operator on the British destroyer Gloucester spotted a Silkworm missile heading for the Missouri. It was shot down with seconds to spare. The Allies high-tech strength on air, sea and land was being borne out. The two armies were virtually three decades apart.

For Saddam's forces the end was near. The Mother of Battles was becoming the Mother of Disasters. The Allies liberated Kuwait City. The Iraqis had fled in panic and disarray, their Generals taking with them stolen Japanese Datsuns and Toyotas. The cars travelled bumper to bumper with the retreating Iraqi armour as the citizens came out on the streets waving flags, singing and chanting in jubilation. It was the end of 207 days of occupation.

American TV reporter Bob MacKeown and his two-man British crew braved Iraqi snipers to become the first journalists into the capital.

The team outpaced the advancing Allies to be hailed heroes by those left in the devastated capital. MacKeown with Londoner's David Green and Andy Thompson raced 50 miles by car along deserted freeways into the city. The reporter, dressed in the battle fatigues of a U.S. major, described scenes of jubilation in a live TV broadcast to a waiting world: "There is no question Kuwait City is free," he shouted. "It's like when Paris was liberated. Those who are left are hugging and kissing each other."

President Bush was among those watching the team's TV pictures of flag-waving Kuwaitis.

As the Kuwaiti army came home to raise their flag hundreds of American tanks and infantry pushed on in the driving rain.

The thrust by the U.S. 7th Corps was on a front dozens of miles wide west of Kuwait. The Iraqis offered stiff resistance but were beaten back. Seven miles from the capital, U.S. marines won a ferocious tank clash around the airport.

Saddam tried to turn the defeat into victory. As air raid sirens sounded in Baghdad, he went on the radio to broadcast:"You have won ... you are victorious. Applaud your victory my dear citizens. You have faced 30 countries and the evil they have brought here. You have faced the whole world, great Iraqis."

But, his army was in almost full retreat and had

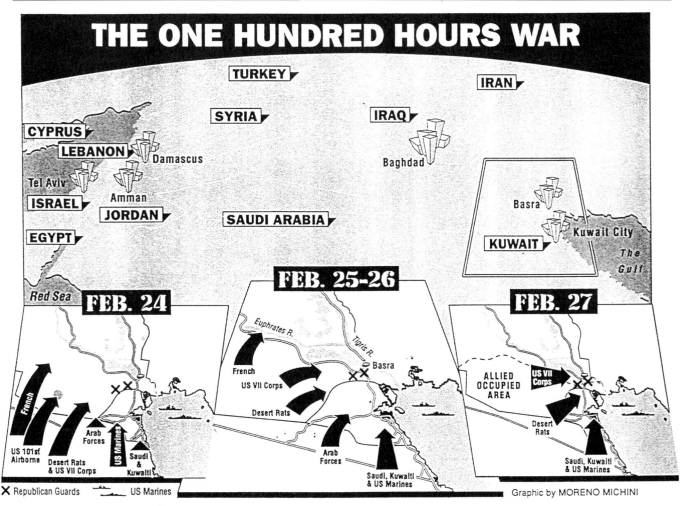

THE ONE HUNDRED HOURS WAR

X Republican Guards   ⟷ US Marines   Graphic by MORENO MICHINI

collapsed across athe field. As the end of the war neared, tragedy struck the Allies. Nine British Desert Rats died in a volley of bullets from a U.S. war plane. It was the worst nightmare realised for the solders' parents, wives and sweethearts waiting for news from the battlefield.

A U.S. A-20 Warthog "tank-busting" fighter had fired armour piercing shells at two British Warrior infantry fighting vehicles "in the heat of the battle." The British troops, most of them teenagers were from the 4th Armoured Brigade attached to the Allied 1st Armoured Division.

They were moving across southern Iraq to the West of the Kuwaiti border in an operation to cut off a retreat by Republican Guard tanks, when the tragedy happened. British commanders vowed history would show they would never be forgotten. The nation mourned its brave Desert Rats. General Schwarzkopf regretted the loss.

The nine victims were: Lee Thompson, a 19-year-old infantryman from Coventry with the 3rd Battalion Royal Regiment of Fusiliers; Private Neil Donald, a marksman with the 1st Battalion of the Queen's Own Highlanders regiment. He came from Forres, Moray; Private John Lang, 19, from Nairn, who was also a rifleman with the Queen's Own Highlanders;

Fusilier Stephen Satchell, 18, from Rye, East Sussex was in the 3rd Battalion of the Royal Regiment of Fusiliers. Proud soldier Conrad Cole from Rochdale, the youngest serviceman to die in the war. He was 17: Martin Ferguson, 21, of Inverlochy, near Fort William wrote a moving poem home to his mother only days before he went into battle; Fusilier Richard Gillespie; Fusilier Kevin Leech, who died in the same a vehicle, celebrated his 20th birthday just days before he was killed; Fusilier Paul Atkinson, 19, from Co Durham.

The remnants of Saddam's Republican Guard were fighting for their lives as the Allied military machine closed in for the kill. Over 800 American tanks and armoured vehicles ploughed across the marshlands west of Basra outflanking and outgunning them as they offered tough, even heroic resistance.

General Schwarzkopf described the armoured duel as a "classic tank battle." But, for the Iraqis, the gates were closed. Thousands of Allied paratroopers dropped deep into Iraq to choke any escape route back to Baghdad.

At 2am on Thursday, February, 28, 100 hours after the land battle had begun, President George Bush appeared on TV to announce to the world

95

Freedom joy: A Kuwaiti waves his national flag along with the Union Jack as his nation is liberated

that the war was over. He had called a ceasefire.

The dramatic seven-and-a-half minute address spoke volumns about his relief and pride in being able to halt the ground war. Although he personally abhored Saddam, he cut out all invective from his victory speech and toned down anything that might suggest he was gloating. His hope was for peace.

The toll was high. At least 100,000 Iraqi soldiers, one in five of Saddam's force, had been killed. Their families would be mourning them as much as the wives and mothers of the Allied soldiers who had died. More than 175,000 were prisoners of war. A total of 126 Allies were killed in action including 17 Britons and 79 Americans.

In Kuwait, there was mounting anger at Iraq's alleged atrocities against civilians. Soldiers were busy screening every Iraqi taken into custody to try and track down those who might be guilty of war crimes.

Allied troops, arriving in Kuwait City also found evidence of Jordanian arms shipped to the Iraqi frontline after the UN embargo.

UN Secretary General Javier Perez de Cuellar sent a special envoy to Baghdad after reports that disease and hunger could kill more Iraqis than the war.

On Monday March 3, Saddam's generals officially surrendered in a tent in the sand. The eight Iraqi officers agreed to every demand of the Allies at an airfield in Safwan, Southern Iraq. All around them was the might of the military machine that destroyed their forces. At their backs was a nation in turmoil, with rebels opposed to Saddam, taking up arms against him.

The Allies first demand was the immediate

release of all prisoners of war. Other conditions of the ceasefire included the release of an estimated 32,000 Kuwaiti hostages still in Iraq, compliance with all UN Security resolutions, payment of war reparations and the renunciation of all territorial claims on Kuwait.

The West's euphoria of victory was heightened when the missing CBS team was freed by the Iraqis after intervention from Mikhail Gorbachev. Hours later ten military prisoners of war were released. Among them was Tornado pilot John Peters, who the Iraqis had paraded on TV. John, sporting a newly grown beard and a beaming smile as he ate chocolates and drank cola, was greeted by diplomats on the Jordanian border. At his side were two British SAS soldiers … and America's sole woman prisoner Melissa Rathbun-Nealy.

The nation held its breath waiting to see if his navigator and friend Adrian Nichol, had also survived captivity. Twenty four hours later the champagne corks popped again as Adrian was handed over to the Red Cross in Baghdad with more freed members of the Allied forces.

The other fliers were Squadron Leader Robert Ankerson, 40; Flt Lts David Waddington, 24; Rupert Clark, 31 and Robert Stewart, 44, and Flying Officer Simon Burgess. They had all taken part in the daring low level raids that won the admiration of military commanders.

But there was agony for the families of five other missing Gulf heroes. Hours of scanning TV news broadcasts and newspaper reports of the conflict in the hope that loved ones would be found were in vain. Relatives were informed they were killed in action.

In the shadow of the pride and joy of seeing Allied forces make ready to come home, the creation of a just and stable peace in the Middle East was now as much a challenge as the invasion of Kuwait. How would President Bush solve the Palestinian problem? The peace, like the war, would have to be dared…but there were no easy options.

As the remnants of Saddam's heavy armour were being used to overthrow an insurrection against him in Basra, Arab states offered to set up a post-war peace keeping force in the Gulf. Syria and Egypt agreed in Damascus to spearhead it.

The conflict had been about people. Ideology had always been a driving force in the world, but those who suffered in the end were the families who lost their sons and daughters.

From the streets of Baghdad, Kuwait and Riyadh to the avenues of Washington, ordinary people paid the price of war. Where would the next war come? Was this the end of the beginning or the beginning of the end?

Daily Express Gulf Reporting Team:
Chris Buckland, Bill Greig, Alun Rees, Ian McKerron, Daniel McGrory, John Ingham, Will Stewart, Nick Assinder, Jack Lee, Alex Hendry, Jane Langston, Nick Buckley, Ted Daly, Paul Thompson, Ashley Walton and Robert McGowan

Sunday Express Gulf Reporting Team:
Ian Henry, Rowena Webster, Bob Graham, Michael Streeter, Alfred Lee and Peter Wilsher

Daily Star Gulf Reporting Team:
John Kierans, Nick Constable, Peter Bond, Barry Gardner, Iain Mayhew, Dick Durham, Peter Welbourn and Amanda Perthen